EASY TO MAKE
KNITTED TOYS

EASY TO MAKE
KNITTED TOYS

Joy Gammon

Series consultant: Eve Harlow

BROCKHAMPTON PRESS
LONDON

KNITTING NEEDLE SIZES

Original UK	000	00	1	2	3	4	5	6	7	8	9	10	11	12	13	14
Metric (mm)	9	$8\frac{1}{2}$	$7\frac{1}{2}$	7	$6\frac{1}{2}$	6	$5\frac{1}{2}$	5	$4\frac{1}{2}$	4	$3\frac{3}{4}$	$3\frac{1}{4}$	3	$2\frac{3}{4}$	$2\frac{1}{4}$	2
USA	15	13	11	$10\frac{1}{2}$	10	9	8	7	6	5	4	3	2	1	0	00

Note: Both imperial and metric measurements are given in patterns. Work to one or the other.

First published in Great Britain in 1990
by Anaya Publishers Ltd, Strode House,
44-50 Osnaburgh Street, London NW1 3ND

This edition published 1996 by Brockhampton Press,
a member of Hodder Headline PLC Group

Editor Eve Harlow
Design Mike Leaman
Photography Di Lewis
Illustrator Kate Simunek
Makes originator Joy Gammon

British Library Cataloguing in Publication Data
A CIP record for this book is available from the British Library

ISBN 1-86019-189-4

Typeset by Tradespools Limited, Frome, Somerset, UK
Colour reproduction by Columbia Offset, Singapore
Printed and bound in EC

CONTENTS

Introduction

Before you begin, read the Safety notes on this page. They are important and will help you to finish the toys more easily and successfully. You will then be satisfied and pleased with the results.

Knitted toys are the nicest kind of all, soft, comforting, washable and practical. They are easy to make, fun to give and easy to love.

Because you make them yourself, knitted toys each have their own character. Also, most patterns can be adapted in different ways so that features, shapes, clothes or colours can be altered. These variations enable you to create completely original and personal toys.

As well as being easy, knitted toys are inexpensive to make; many of those in this book are made from scraps of yarn that might be found in your yarn basket. But although they are inexpensive gifts, the most important thing you give is your time and care – and that's the best gift of all. Some of the toys in this book are easy enough for children to knit for themselves, with a little help from you. And what a lovely way to begin to knit!

Safety notes

When making toys for children, it is vitally important that the materials used are safe. Filling must be non-flammable and, for practical reasons, washable and lightweight. Plastic eyes and noses should be the safety kind and trimmings and ribbons must be firmly stitched on.

For very young children, it is best not to sew on any decorations at all, but use embroidery. Make sure that all toy pieces are firmly sewn together. Keep small toys for older children – there is always the danger that small children will try to swallow them. Bigger toys are best for children under three years old.

Tension

Most of the toys in this book are worked in double knitting yarn, with the same basic tension, as follows:

> 24 stitches and 30 rows to 4in (10cm) in stocking stitch on 4mm/No 8 needles.

It is recommended that before you start, you work a piece of knitting in DK yarn to this tension, using the needles specified. You may find that you knit tightly and have to use a larger size needle to obtain the tension, or knit loosely and have to use a smaller size needle. When you have discovered the correct needle size for you, you can use those needles for most of the patterns in this book, where double knitting yarn is specified. Patterns which use other thicknesses of yarn give a special tension.

STANDARD ABBREVIATIONS

beg = begin(ning)
cont = continue
dec = decrease
foll = follow(ing)
inc = increase
k = knit
p = purl
patt = pattern

psso = pass slip st over
rem = remain(ing)
sl = slip
st(s) = stitch(es)
st st = stocking stitch
tbl = through back of
loop
tog = together
yon = yarn over needle

BRITISH AND AMERICAN KNITTING TERMS

UK	US
Stocking stitch	= Stockinette stitch
Tension	= Gauge
Work straight	= Work even
Cast off	= Bind off
Yarn over needle	= Yarn over

Making up toys

When you have knitted all the pieces for your toy, the pattern instructions tell you how to stitch the pieces together, stuff the toy, finish and decorate it. If the toy is an unusual shape, a diagram will have been provided to help you fit the pieces together. It is a good idea also to study the picture of the toy as this is your best guide to the way in which it should be put together.

Seaming

When sewing larger pieces together, use a stretching stitch, such as back stitch, matching any shaping or colours. On small pieces, where there is insufficient room for back stitching, or when you are sewing two stuffed pieces together, oversew as neatly and as invisibly as possible. If a thread has been run through the stitches at the end of the work, draw this tightly and use the thread to seam, gathering the stitches closed. With spherical or egg-shaped pieces, the casting-on can be gathered too, to create a neat finish.
If the making-up instructions say 'attach open ended', this means that the piece (for example, an animal's leg) is seamed except for the top, stuffed and then attached to the body at the open top.

Stuffing toys

Use a washable, lightweight, white acrylic toy filling. Avoid heavy fillings, especially for the larger toys. I prefer my toys soft and cuddly and I stuff them fairly lightly. If you prefer a toy more firmly stuffed, it is a good idea to knit the pieces on smaller needles to give a firmer fabric which will not stretch out of shape so easily.
Safety toy eyes and noses are inserted into the knitted fabric before stuffing. Check that they are in the right place before finally securing them because, of course, they are very difficult to remove.

Embroidery

The success of a toy depends on its features and expression. Look carefully at the pictures of the toy you are making and try and copy the embroidery as closely as possible. You can, of course, work the features in your own way and thus achieve a special and unique expression and character. Use back stitch for thin, straight lines and chain stitch for thicker lines, dots and larger areas of colour.
Dolls and animals have very different and distinctive mouths and eyes. Some shapes are given on pages 20 and 40 to help you with your embroidery.

1: PEOPLE

Baby doll and layette

This doll is the perfect present for a small amount of cost, but lots of time and love. You can create a gift that any child would appreciate.

Materials
Baby doll: 2 (50g) balls Sirdar Country Style Double Knitting in peach; oddments for embroidery; pair of 4mm/No 8 knitting needles; washable polyester toy filling.
Layette: 5 (50g) balls Sirdar Country Style 4 ply, in white; pair of 3¼mm/No 10 knitting needles; 1⅛yd (1m) of ¼in (6mm)-wide velvet ribbon; 1⅝yd (1.5m) of ¾in (18mm)-wide satin ribbon; 10 ribbon roses; 6 transparent press fasteners; safety pin (optional).
Measurements
Baby doll: approx 14in (36cm) long.
Clothes: to fit a doll approx 14in (36cm) long with a chest measurement of approx 11in (28cm).
Tension
24 sts and 30 rows to 4in (10cm) measured over st st on 4mm/No 8 needles and DK.
30 sts and 38 rows to 4in (10cm) measured over st st on 3¼mm/No 10 needles and 4 ply.

BABY DOLL

Body (make 1)
Cast on 4 sts.
* Working in st st throughout, work as follows:
Next row (wrong side): P.
Next row: Inc knitwise in every st * – 8 sts.
Rep these 2 rows until there are 64 sts.
Work 27 rows straight, so ending p row.
** **Next row:** (K2 tog) to end.
Next row: P ** – 32 sts.
Rep these 2 rows until 4 sts remain. Run a thread through rem sts.

Head (make 1)
Cast on 9 sts. Work as given for body from * to * until there are 72 sts.
Work 19 rows straight, so ending p row.
Work as for body from ** to ** until 9 sts rem. Cast off.

Legs and feet (make 2)
Cast on 8 sts. Work as given for body from * to * until there are 32 sts.
Next row: P.
Next row: K12, inc knitwise in next 8 sts, k12 – 40 sts.
Next row: P.
Next row: K16, inc knitwise in next 8 sts, k16 – 48 sts.
Work 5 rows, so ending p row.
Next row: K16, (k2 tog) 8 times, k16 – 40 sts.
Next row: P.
Next row: K12, (k2 tog) 8 times, k12 – 32 sts.
Work 11 rows, so ending p row.

Shape knee:
*** **Next row:** K21, turn, sl 1, p to end.
Next row: K.
Next row: P21, turn, sl 1, k to end.
Next row: P ***.
Rep these 4 rows once more.
Work 10 rows straight, so ending p row.
Cast off 4 sts at beg of every row until 4 sts rem. Cast off.

Arms (make 2)
Cast on 2 sts.
Beg k row and working in st st, inc 1 st each end of every row to 32 sts.
Work 11 rows, so ending p row.

Shape elbow:
Work as given for legs from *** to ***.
Work 10 rows, so ending p row.
Work as given for body from ** to ** until 4 sts rem. Run a thread through rem sts.

Finishing
Join body seam, leaving an opening, fill, close opening. Join legs and feet seams, matching shaping, fill and attach open ended. Join arms seams, fill and attach open

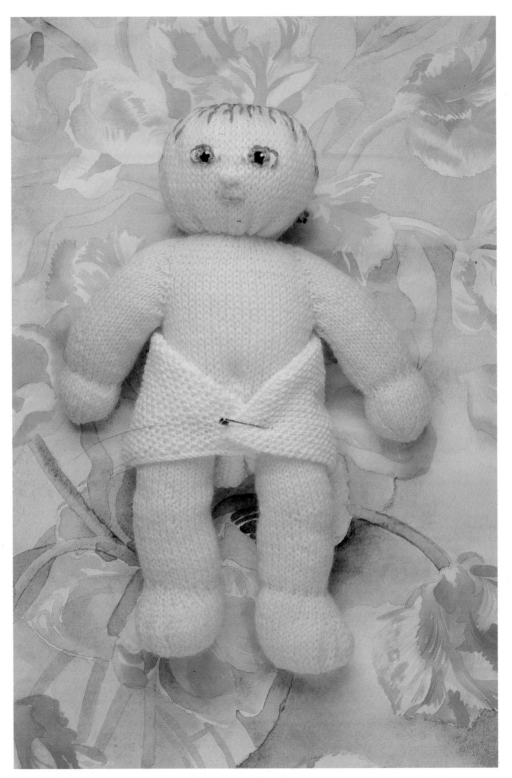

ended. Run a gathering thread lightly around each wrist and ankle. Join head seam, leaving an opening, fill, close opening and attach to body. Run a gathering thread around a ½in (12mm) diameter circle in the centre of the face and pull tight to form a nose. Embroider navel, hair and features (see picture).

LAYETTE

ALL-IN-ONE-SUIT

Right leg
Cast on 12 sts.

* Working in st st, work as follows:
Next row (wrong side): P.
Next row: Inc knitwise in every st* – 24 sts.
Rep these 2 rows once more – 48 sts.
Work straight until leg measures 5in (13cm) from cast on edge, ending k row. Break off yarn and leave sts on a holder.

Left leg
Work as given for right leg, but do not break off yarn.

Body
With wrong side facing, p across 48 sts of left leg, then 48 sts of right leg – 96 sts.

Cast on 2 sts at beg of next 2 rows – 100 sts.
Cont in st st, but work 2 sts at each end of
every row in k to form a garter st front
opening edge.
Work a further 3½in (9cm) straight, ending p
row.

** Shape raglan:
Next row: K24, k2 tog tbl, turn and leave
rem sts on a holder, p to last 2 sts, k2.
Work on these sts only for right front.
*** Keeping garter st edge correct, dec 1 st
at inside (armhole edge) on next, then every
foll alt row until 20 sts rem, then on every
row until 8 sts rem.
Work 1 row, so ending wrong side row ***.
Do not break off yarn, leave sts on a holder.
Rejoin yarn to inside edge of rem sts, k2 tog,
k44, k2 tog tbl, turn, leaving rem sts on a
holder, p to end. Work on these sts only for
back.
Dec 1 st each end of next, then every foll alt
row until 36 sts rem, then on every row until
12 sts rem.
Work 1 row, so ending p row. Leave sts on a
holder.
Rejoin yarn to inside edge of rem sts, k2 tog,
k to end. Work on these sts only for left
front.
Next row: K2, p to end.
Rep from *** to *** and leave sts on a
holder **.

Sleeves (make 2)
Cast on 6 sts.
Work as given for legs from * to * until there
are 48 sts.
Work straight until sleeve measures 4in
(10cm) from cast on edge, ending p row.
**** Shape raglan: Dec 1 st each end of
every alt row until 40 sts rem, then every
row until 6 sts remain.
Work 1 row, so ending p row. Leave sts on a
holder ****.

Neckband
Join all raglan seams matching shaping.
With right side facing and using attached
yarn, k across 8 sts of right front, 6 sts of right
sleeve head, 12 sts of back neck, 6 sts of left
sleeve head, then 8 sts of left front – 40 sts.
K 3 rows.
Cast off loosely.

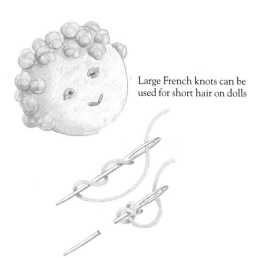

Large French knots can be
used for short hair on dolls

Finishing
Join inside leg seams, then front opening for
¾in (2cm). Join sleeve seams, then set in
sleeves. Sew press fasteners to front opening.

MATINÉE JACKET

Main piece (knitted in one to armholes)
Cast on 196 sts and work picot edge:
Row 1: K.
Row 2: P.
Row 3: K.
Row 4: P.
Row 5: K2, (yon, k2 tog) to last 2 sts, k2.
Next row: K2, p to last 2, k2.
Next row: K.
Rep the last 2 rows until work measures 4in
(10cm) from cast on edge, ending k row.
Next row: K2, (p2 tog) to last 2 sts, k2
–100 sts.
Shape raglan: Work as for All-in-one suit
from ** to **.

Sleeves
Cast on 48 sts and work the 5 rows of picot
edge as given for main piece of matinée
jacket.
Beg p row, work in st st until sleeve measures
3½in (9cm) from cast on edge, ending p row.
Shape raglan: Work as for All-in-one suit
from **** to ****.

Neckband
Work as given for the neckband of the All-
in-one suit.

13

Finishing

Join sleeve seams. Turn picot edge to wrong side and loosely slip st in place.
Sew press fasteners to front opening of yoke. Decorate with 2 ribbon roses.

Nappy

Cast on 61 sts.
Row 1: K1, (pl, k1) to end.
This row forms the moss st patt.
Cont in patt until nappy measures approx 8in (20cm) (or square).
Cast off loosely.

Finishing

Fold in the traditional way and either fasten with a safety pin or, if the toy is for a young child, work a few stitches to hold in place and embroider a safety pin shape on the front.

Bonnet

Cast on 60 sts.
Work the 5 rows of picot edge as given for main piece of matinée jacket.
Beg p row, work in st st until bonnet measures 4in (10cm) from cast on edge ending k row.
Next row: K.
Shape back:
Next row: (K2 tog, k11, k2 tog tbl) 4 times – 52 sts.
Next and every foll alt row: P.
Next K row: (K2 tog, k9, k2 tog tbl) 4 times – 44 sts.
Next K row: (K2 tog, k7, k2 tog tbl) 4 times – 36 sts.
Next K row: (K2 tog, k5, k2 tog tbl) 4 times – 28 sts.
Next K row: (K2 tog, k3, k2 tog tbl) 4 times – 20 sts.
Next K row: (K2 tog, k1, k2 tog tbl) 4 times – 12 sts.
Next row: P.
Next row: (Sl 1, k2 tog, psso) 4 times.
Run a thread through rem 4 sts.

Finishing

Join shaped edges together, leaving straight edges open. Turn picot edge to wrong side

and loosely slip st in place. Sew a length of velvet ribbon, caught with a ribbon rose, to the corners of sides. (The picot edge can be worn round the face or at the back neck.)

Bootees

Cast on 48 sts and work the 5 rows of picot edge as given for main piece of matinée jacket.
Beg p row, work in st st until bootee measures 2in (5cm) from cast on edge, ending p row.
Next row: K18, inc knitwise in next 12 sts, k18 – 60 sts.
Next row: P.
Next row: K24, inc knitwise in next 12 sts, k24 – 72 sts.
Work 7 rows straight.
Next row: K24, (k2 tog) 12 times, k24 – 60 sts.
Next row: P.
Next row: K18, (k2 tog) 12 times, k18 – 48 sts.
Next row: P.
Next row: (K2 tog) to end – 24 sts.
Next row: P.
Rep last 2 rows once more – 12 sts.
Cast off.

Finishing

Fold cast off edge in half and seam, then join row ends as a back seam. Turn picot edge to wrong side and loosely sew in place.
Thread a velvet ribbon through the knitting at the ankle and tie in a bow at the front.
Sew on a ribbon rose.

Shawl

Cast on 97 sts.
Row 1: K2, (yon, k2 tog) to last st, k1.
Row 2: P.
Row 3: K1, (yon, k2 tog) to end.
Row 4: P.
Rep these 4 rows until shawl is square.
Cast off loosely.

Finishing

Crochet a picot edge around the complete shawl. On each corner, sew on a satin ribbon bow and ribbon rose.

Small figures

Small figures

The basic pattern here makes a small doll with six variations. You can adapt the instructions to make any figures you like, a sports team, scouts and guides, characters from a story, your family or friends.

Materials
Sirdar Double Knitting; small quantities of contrast colours as stated for each variation; oddments for embroidery and assorted trims; pair of 4mm/No 8 knitting needles; washable polyester toy filling.

Measurement
Approx 5in (13cm) tall.
Tension
24 sts and 30 rows to 4in (10cm) measured over st st on 4mm/No 8 needles.

BASIC DOLL

Main piece
First leg: Cast on 3 sts.
* Working in st st, work as follows:
Next row (wrong side): P.
Next row: Inc knitwise in every st * – 6 sts.
Rep from * to * once more – 12 sts.
Work 12 rows straight, so ending k row.
Leave sts on a holder and break off yarn.
Second leg: Work as given for first leg but do not break off yarn.

Body
With wrong side facing, p across 12 sts of second leg, then p across 12 sts of first leg – 24 sts.
Work 14 rows straight, so ending p row.

Shape neck and head
** **Next row:** (K2 tog) to end.
Next row: P ** – 12 sts.
Rep from ** to ** once more – 6 sts.
Next row: Inc knitwise in every st – 12 sts.
Work 7 rows straight, so ending p row.
Rep from ** to ** – 6 sts.
Run a thread through rem sts.

Arms (make 2)
Cast on 2 sts.
Beg k row and working in st st, inc 1 st each end of every row to 12 sts.
Work 11 rows straight, so ending p row.
Rep from ** to ** as given for main piece until 3 sts rem.
Run a thread through rem sts.

Finishing
Join legs, body and head seam, matching colours and leaving an opening, fill and close opening. Join arm seams, fill and attach to shoulders.

TENNIS PLAYER

Main piece
Using white, cast on each leg and work inc rows and first 6 rows of st st, then complete each leg in peach, now work body and first 4 rows of neck shaping in white, complete in peach.

Arms
Using white, cast on and work inc rows and first 3 rows straight, complete in peach.

Finishing
Complete figure as basic figure. Embroider detail and features (see picture). Add hair and 'sweat band' cords.

WALKER

Main piece
Using brown, cast on each leg and work inc rows and first 2 rows straight, then work 4 rows red, 4 rows peach, last 2 rows of leg and first 7 rows of body in dark green, then complete straight rows and first 4 rows of neck shaping in pale yellow, complete in peach.

Arms
Using pale yellow, cast on and work inc rows and first 3 rows straight in pale yellow, then complete in peach.

Hat (make 1)
Using dark green, cast on 18 sts and work 2 rows in k1, p1 rib.
Next row: (K2 tog) to end – 12 sts.
Next row: P.
Next row: (K2 tog) to end – 6 sts.
Run a thread through rem sts and use to seam.
Bobble
Using red, cast on 1 st and work 4 times knitwise into this st.
Next row: P.
Next row: K.
Next row: P4 tog, fasten off.
Attach to top of hat.

Scarf (make 1)
Using red, cast on 30 sts, then cast off.

Finishing
Complete figure as basic figure. Sew on hat and add hair. Embroider features (see picture) and a belt around the waist. Tie on the scarf.

BALLET DANCER

Legs, body and head
Using white, cast on each leg and work inc rows and first 2 rows straight, then complete each leg in peach, now work body and first 4 rows of neck shaping in pink, complete in peach.

Arms
In peach throughout.

Tutu (make 1)
Using pink, cast on 72 sts and k 4 rows. Beg k row and working in st st, work 10 rows, so ending p row.

Next row: (K3 tog) to end – 24 sts.
Next row: Work 3 times knitwise in every st – 72 sts.
Beg p row, and so reversing the right side of the fabric, work 8 rows, so ending k row.
K 4 rows.
Cast off loosely.

Finishing
Complete figure as basic figure. Join seams of tutu. Double at centre decreasing, gather around waist and attach. Add hair, embroider features and decorate (see picture).

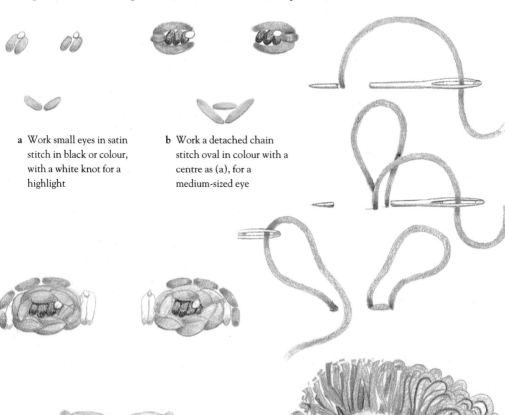

a Work small eyes in satin stitch in black or colour, with a white knot for a highlight

b Work a detached chain stitch oval in colour with a centre as (a), for a medium-sized eye

c For a large eye, work a black pupil in straight stiches, with white knot as (a), then work colour round and outline in black chain stitch

20

BRIDE

Main piece
Using white, cast on each leg and work inc rows and first 2 rows straight, then complete each leg in peach, now work body and first 4 rows of neck shaping in white, complete in peach.

Arms
Using white, cast on and work inc rows and first 8 rows straight, then complete in peach.

Skirt (make 1)
Using white, cast on 72 sts and work picot hem:
Row 1: K.
Row 2: P.
Row 3: K2, (yon, k2 tog) to end.
Row 4: P.
Beg k row and working in st st, work until skirt measures 2½in (6cm) from cast on edge, ending p row.
Next row: (K2 tog) to end.
Cast off.

Finishing
Complete figure as basic figure. Join skirt seam. Turn picot hem to wrong side and slip st in place. Gather cast off edge and attach to waist of doll. Decorate skirt, add hair and a net or lace veil. Make and sew to hand a bouquet of ribbon roses. Embroider features (see picture).

GROOM

Main piece
Using black, cast on each leg and work inc rows and first 2 rows straight, then complete legs, body and first 2 rows of neck shaping in grey, now work next 3 rows of neck shaping in white and complete in peach.

Arms
Using grey, cast on and work inc rows and first 8 rows straight, then complete in peach.

Finishing
Complete figure as basic figure. Embroider black lines of suit jacket, white shirt collar, coloured tie and hanky. Embroider features (see picture), add hair and sew a ribbon rose to lapel.

Stitch long lengths of yarn from the centre parting, draw back and style

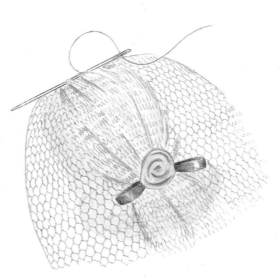

Gather net edge for a veil, sew to the head

23

CAVEMAN

Work main piece and arms in peach throughout, except for first 6 rows of body after leg join, which is worked in brown.

Leopard skin (make 1)
Using bright yellow, cast on 16 sts.
Beg k row and working in st st, inc 1 st each end of every row to 32 sts.
Work 4 rows.
Next row: K2 tog, k14, turn and leave rem sts on a holder.

** Dec 1 st at outside edge of every row until 6 sts rem.
Cast off **.
Rejoin yarn to inside edge of rem sts, k to last 2 sts, k2 tog.
Rep from ** to **.

Finishing
Complete figure as basic figure. Join cast off edges and side edges of leopard skin to form shoulder and side seams respectively. Embroider with black spots. Add hair and embroider features (see picture).

By changing colours and clothes, eyes, mouths and hair the basic doll could be a hiker, pirate, clown or angel for the Christmas tree, or costume characters, such as a Victorian couple

Large dolls

The pattern is for a basic figure which, with the addition of skirts and frills, or shorts, boots or socks, or space suit and helmet, make a Pop Queen, Gipsy, Astronaut or Footballer. You can make more character dolls by varying the colours, clothes and details.

Measurement
Approx 14in (36cm) tall.
Tension
24 sts and 30 rows to 4in (10cm) measured over st st on 4mm/No 8 needles.

BASIC FIGURE PATTERN
Main body and leg piece (make 1)

Left leg and foot
Cast on 12 sts.
Working in st st, work as follows:
Next row (wrong side): P.
Next row: Inc knitwise in every st – 24 sts.
Next row: P.
Next row: K15, inc knitwise in next 6 sts, k3 – 30 sts.
Next row: P.
Next row: K18, inc knitwise in next 6 sts, k6 – 36 sts.
Work 5 rows.
Next row: K18, (k2 tog) 6 times, k6 – 30 sts.
Next row: P.
Next row: K15, (k2 tog) 6 times, k3 – 24 sts.
Work a further 3½in (9cm) straight, ending k row.
Break off yarn and leave sts on a holder.

Right leg and foot
Cast on 12 sts.
Working in st st, work as follows:
Next row (wrong side): P.
Next row: Inc knitwise in every st – 24 sts.
Next row: P.
Next row: K3, inc knitwise in next 6 sts, k15 – 30 sts.
Next row: P.
Next row: K6, inc knitwise in next 6 sts, k18 – 36 sts.

Work 5 rows.
Next row: K6, (k2 tog) 6 times, k18 – 30 sts.
Next row: P.
Next row: K3, (k2 tog) 6 times, k15 – 24 sts.
Work a further 3½in (9cm) straight, ending k row.
Do not break off yarn.

Body
With wrong side facing, p across 24 sts of right leg, then p across 24 sts of left leg – 48 sts.
Work a further 5in (13cm) straight, ending p row.
Shape shoulders:
Next row: K12, turn and working on these sts only, cast off 3 sts, p to end.
Next row: K.
Next row: Cast off 3 sts, p to end.
Cast off rem 6 sts.
Rejoin yarn to inside edge of rem sts, cast off 3 sts, k 21 sts, turn and working on these sts only, cast off 3 sts at beg of next 3 rows.
Cast off rem 12 sts.
Rejoin yarn to inside edge of rem sts, cast off 3 sts and k to end.
Next row: P.
Next row: Cast off 3 sts, k to end.
Cast off rem 6 sts.

Arms (make 2)
Cast on 2 sts.
Beg k row and working in st st, inc 1 st each end of every row to 24 sts.
Work a further 3in (8cm) straight, ending p row.
** Next row: (K2 tog, k8, k2 tog tbl) twice – 20 sts.
Next row: (P2 tog tbl, p6, p2 tog) twice – 16 sts.

Next row: (K2 tog, k4, k2 tog tbl) twice – 12 sts.
Next row: (P2 tog tbl, p2, p2 tog) twice – 8 sts.
Cast off.

Head (make 1)
Cast on 5 sts.
Working in st st, work as follows:

Next row (wrong side): P.
Next row: Inc knitwise in every st – 10 sts.
Rep the last 2 rows until there are 40 sts.
Work 15 rows straight, so ending p row.
Next row: (K2 tog) to end.
Next row: P.
Rep these 2 rows until 5 sts rem. Run a thread through rem sts.

29

Finishing

Join leg, centre back, top shoulder and neck seams, leaving an opening, fill, close opening. Join arms seams, fill and attach open ended by decreased top edge to shoulders. Join head seam, fill and attach. Embroider and dress as for chosen doll.

ASTRONAUT

Materials

1 (50g) ball Sirdar Wash 'n' Wear Crepe Double Knitting in each of peach (skin colour) and pale grey; part balls in white and dark grey; oddments of yarn for embroidery; pair of 4mm/No 8 knitting needles; washable polyester toy filling; 5 transparent press fasteners.

Legs, body, arms and head

Using peach, work as given in the basic pattern.

Boots (make 2)

*** Using white, cast on 14 sts.
Working in st st, work as follows:
Next row (wrong side): P.
Next row: Inc knitwise in every st – 28 sts.
Next row: P.
Next row: K11, inc knitwise in next 6 sts, k11 – 34 sts.
Next row: P.
Next row: K13, inc knitwise in next 8 sts, k13 – 42 sts.
Work 5 rows.
Next row: K13, (k2 tog) 8 times, k13 – 34 sts.
Next row: P.
Next row: K11, (k2 tog) 6 times, k11 – 28 sts ***.
Work 1½in (4cm) straight, ending p row.
Work 3 rows in k1, p1, rib.
Cast off in rib.

Gloves (make 2)

Using white, cast on 26 sts and work 4 rows in k1, p1 rib.
Beg k row, work in st st until glove measures 2⅜in (6cm) from cast on edge, ending p row and dec 1 st each end of last row – 24 sts.

Work as for arms of basic figure pattern for large doll from ** to end.

Suit (main piece, make 1)
First leg (making hem)

Using pale grey, cast on 27 sts.
Beg k row, work 3 rows in st st.
Next row: K.
Beg k row, work 5 rows in st st.
Next row: K.
Beg k row, work a further 2½in (6cm) straight, ending k row.
Break off yarn.

Second leg

Work as given for first leg, but do not break off yarn.

Body

Next row: With wrong side facing, p across 27 sts of first leg, then across 27 sts of second leg – 54 sts.
Work 3in (8cm) straight, ending p row.
Shape armholes:
Next row: K13, turn, leaving rem sts on a holder, p2 tog tbl, p to end.
*** Dec 1 st at inside (armhole) edge on every foll alt row until 6 sts rem.
Work 1 row.
Cast off ***.
Rejoin yarn to inside edge of rem sts, k2 tog, k24, k2 tog tbl, turn leaving rem sts on a holder.
Dec 1 st each end of every foll alt row until 12 sts rem.
Cast off.
Rejoin yarn to inside edge of rem sts and k to end.
Next row: P to last 2 sts, p2 tog.
Rep from *** to ***.

Sleeves (make 2)

Using pale grey, cast on 26 sts and work 2 rows in k1, p1 rib.
Beg k row, work in st st until sleeve measures 2⅜in (6cm) from cast on edge, ending p row.
Dec 1 st each end of next, then every alt row until 12 sts rem.
Work 1 row.
Cast off.

Helmet (make 1)

Using pale grey, cast on 40 sts and work 4 rows in k1, p1 rib.
Beg k row, work 16 rows in st st.
Next row: (K2 tog) to end – 20 sts.
Next row: P.
Rep these 2 rows until 5 sts rem, then run a thread through rem sts.

Back pack (make 1)

Using dark grey, cast on 12 sts.
Beg k row, work 7 rows in st st.
Next row: Cast on 6 sts at beg of row, k to end.
Rep the last row once more – 24 sts.
Work 3in (8cm) straight, ending p row.
Next row: Cast off 6 sts at beg of row, k to end.
Rep last row once more – 12 sts.
Beg k row, work 7 rows in st st.
Cast off.

Waist strap (make 1)

Using dark grey, cast on 60 sts and work 4 rows in k1, p1 rib.
Cast off in rib.

Shoulder straps (make 2)

Using dark grey, work as given for waist strap, but cast on 30 sts.

Air tube (make 1)

Using white, cast on 12 sts.
Next row: K.
Next row: P.
Next row: P.
Next row: K.
Rep these 4 rows until work measures 6in (15cm).
Cast off.

Finishing

Complete figure as basic figure. **Suit:** Join leg seams and bottom 1in (2.5cm) of front seam. Join sleeve seams, then sew to main piece. Turn trouser bottom hems to wrong side and loosely slip st in place. Evenly join cast on edge of helmet around complete neck edge. Close front opening with 3 press fasteners. Form back pack into a box by joining corner seams, fill and attach by open side to centre back of suit immediately below helmet. Sew waist strap around suit immediately below back pack overlapping the front ends and closing with 2 press fasteners. Sew on shoulder straps from top corners of back pack to top of waist strap at front. Join air tube seam and attach one end to side of helmet and other end to back pack. Join foot and back seams of boots. Join side seams of gloves. Sew on very short brown hair and embroider features (see picture).

FOOTBALLER

Materials

1 (50g) ball Sirdar Wash 'n' Wear Crepe Double Knitting in beige (skin colour); part balls in each of scarlet, royal blue, white and black; oddments of yarn for embroidery; pair of 4mm/No 8 knitting needles; washable polyester toy filling.

Legs, body, arms and head

Using beige, work as given in basic pattern.

Shorts

Using white, work as for Pop Queen.

Shirt

Work as for Pop Queen, but work back and front in royal blue, sleeves in red and make all pieces 2½in (6cm) straight before decreasing.

Socks

Work as for Astronaut boots, but in white with last st st row and top rib in royal blue.

Boots

Using black only, work as for Astronaut boots from *** to *** only.
Cast off.

Finishing

Complete figure as basic figure. Complete shorts and shirt as for Pop Queen. Complete socks as for Astronaut's boots. **Boots:** Join foot and back seam, leaving complete cast off edge as boot top. Sew on white laces, winding a length twice around each foot and finishing with a bow. Embroider hair and features (see picture).

POP QUEEN

Materials

1 (50g) ball Sirdar Country Style Double Knitting in peach (skin colour); part balls in bright pink and jade; oddments of yarn for hair and embroidery; pair of 4mm/No 8 knitting needles; quantity of silver sequins for decoration; washable polyester toy filling.

Legs and body

Using bright pink and working from basic figure pattern, cast on and work feet and first 2in (5cm) of each leg, then complete in peach.

Arms and head

Using peach, work as given in basic pattern.

Shorts (make 1)

Using jade, cast on 50 sts and k 4 rows. Beg k row and working in st st, work until

shorts measure 2in (5cm) from cast on edge.
Work 4 rows k1, p1 rib.
Cast off in rib.
Join row ends together to form centre back
seam, then catch cast on edge together at
centre to form two leg openings.

Shirt
Back (make 1)
Using bright pink, cast on 26 sts and work 2
rows in k1, p1 rib.
Beg k row, work in st st until work measures
1½in (4cm) from cast on edge, ending p row.
Shape armholes:
Dec 1 st each end of next, then every foll alt
row until 12 sts rem. Work 1 row.
Cast off.
Front (make 1)
Work as given for back.
Sleeves (make 2)
Work as given for back but work only ¾in
(2cm) straight before commencing armhole
shaping.

Finishing
Complete figure as basic figure. Join side,
sleeve and raglan seams, matching shaping.
Decorate shirt and shorts with sequins. Sew
sequins to one boot, wrist and ears to form a
bracelet and earrings. Sew on pale yellow
hair and embroider features (see picture).

GIPSY

Materials
1 (50g) ball Sirdar Country Style Double
Knitting in each of dark beige (skin colour)
and dark red; part balls in each of scarlet and
black; oddments of yarn for hair and
embroidering; pair of 4mm/No 8 knitting
needles; small quantity of gold thread;
ribbon rose or similar; short length of elastic;
washable polyester toy filling.

Legs, body, arms and head
Using dark beige, work as given in basic
pattern.

Pants
Using bright red, work as given for Pop
Queen's shorts.

Shirt
Using black, work as for Pop Queen's shirt.

Skirt
Frills
Using bright red, cast on 216 sts.
K 10 rows.
Next row: (K2 tog) to end – 108 sts.
Break off yarn and leave these sts on a spare
needle.
Using darker red, cast on 216 sts.
K 8 rows.

Next row: (K2 tog) to end – 108 sts.
Next row: Place needle with bright
red frill behind needle with dark red frill,
both needles facing to the right, using
dark red, k together 1 st from each needle to
end – 108 sts.
Beg p row, work in st st for a further 6in
(15cm), ending p row.
Next row: (K2 tog) to end – 54 sts.
Work 4 rows in k1, p1 rib.
Cast off in rib.

Shawl
Using bright red, cast on 1 st.
Row 1: Work 3 times knitwise into this st –
3 sts.
Row 2 and every alt row: P.
Row 3: K1, yon, k1, yon, k1.
Row 5: K1, yon, (k2 tog, yon) to last 2 sts,
k1, yon, k1 – 7 sts.
Row 7: K1, yon, k1, (yon, k2 tog) to last st,
yon, k1 – 9 sts.
Row 8: P.
Rep rows 5 to 8 until work measures 5in
(13cm) from cast on st, so ending p row.
Cast off.

Finishing
Complete figure as basic figure. Complete
pants and shirt as Pop Queen's. Join row
ends of bright red frill, then row ends of dark
red frill and straight section. Cut elastic to fit
waist, join into a ring, and work herringbone
st over elastic to wrong side of skirt waist.
Fringe short edges of shawl. With gold
thread, embroider bracelets, anklet and
earring. Sew on long black hair and catch to
one side with ribbon rose. Embroider
features (see picture).

2: A FAMILY OF BEARS

Traditional teddy

This is everyone's favourite Edwardian bear with the traditional long nose and curved arms. He's made in a tough, washable Aran yarn, so that he will last as long as his forebears.

Materials
3 (50g) balls Sirdar Wash 'n' Wear Aran in mink brown; oddments of yarn for embroidery; pair of 4mm/No 8 knitting needles; 1 pair toy safety eyes; washable polyester toy filling.
Measurements
Approx 14in (36cm) long.
Tension
18 sts and 24 rows to 4in (10cm) measured over st st on 4mm/No 8 needles.

Body (make 1)
Cast on 9 sts.
* Working in st st, work as follows:
Next row (wrong side): P.
Next row: Inc knitwise in every st * – 18 sts.
Rep from * to * until there are 72 sts.
Work straight until body measures 7in (18cm), ending p row.
** **Next row:** (K2 tog) to end.
Next row: P ** – 36 sts.
Rep from ** to ** until 9 sts rem.
Run a thread through rem sts.

Head (make 1)
Cast on 7 sts.
Work as given for body from * to * until there are 56 sts.
Work 15 rows straight.
Shape top:
Next row: (K2 tog, k10, k2 tog tbl) 4 times – 48 sts.
Next row: (P2 tog tbl, p8, p2 tog) 4 times – 40 sts.
Next row: (K2 tog, k6, k2 tog tbl) 4 times – 32 sts.
Next row: (P2 tog tbl, p4, p2 tog) 4 times – 24 sts.
Next row: (K2 tog, k2, k2 tog tbl) 4 times – 16 sts.

Next row: (P2 tog tbl, p2 tog) 4 times – 8 sts.
Run a thread through rem sts.

Arms (make 2)
Cast on 7 sts. Work as given for body from * to * until there are 28 sts.
Work 17 rows straight, so ending p row.
Shape elbow:
Next row: K18, turn, sl 1, p7, turn, sl 1, k to end.
Next row: P20, turn, sl 1, k11, turn, sl 1, p to end.
Rep the first of these 2 rows once more.
Work 17 rows straight, so ending p row.
Work as given for body from ** to ** until 7 sts rem.
Run a thread through rem sts.

Legs and feet (make 2)
Cast on 7 sts. Work as given for body from * to * until there are 28 sts.
Work 1 row.
Next row: K10, inc knitwise in next 8 sts, k10 – 36 sts.
Next row: P.
Next row: K14, inc knitwise in next 8 sts, k14 – 44 sts.
Work 5 rows straight.
Next row: K14, (k2 tog) 8 times, k14 – 36 sts.
Next row: P.
Next row: K10, (k2 tog) 8 times, k10 – 28 sts.
Beg p row, work a further 3½in (9cm) straight, ending p row.
Next row: (K2 tog) to end – 14 sts.
Cast off.

Muzzle (make 1)
Cast on 36 sts.
Beg k row and working in st st, work 2in

(5cm) straight, ending p row.
Work as given for body from ** to ** until 9
sts rem.
Run a thread through rem sts.

Ears (make 2)
Cast on 10 sts.
Beg k row and working in st st, work 6 rows.
Next row: K2 tog, k6, k2 tog tbl – 8 sts.
Next row: P2 tog tbl, p4, p2 tog – 6 sts.
Inc 1 st each end of next 2 rows – 10 sts.
Work 6 rows.
Cast off.

Finishing
Join body seam leaving an opening, fill,
close opening. Join arm and leg seams,
closing seams completely after filling and
attach. Join head seam, insert toy safety
eyes, fill and attach with shaped decreasing
as the top.

Join sides of muzzle, fill and attach
open ended to front of head by cast on
edge. Double ears, join sides and attach with
bases curved to give shape. Embroider
traditional teddy nose and mouth (see
page 40).

Modern teddy

Modern teddies have become fatter, more cuddly and tend to have less defined arms and legs. Today's bears even wear clothes sometimes, although this modern teddy sports just a large, checked bow.

Materials

1 (100g) ball Sirdar Country Style Chunky in beige; small quantity of cream; oddments of Double Knitting for embroidery; pair of 6½mm/No 3 knitting needles; 1 pair of toy safety eyes; washable polyester toy filling; length of ribbon.

Measurements
Approx 15in (38cm) long.

Tension
14 sts and 19 rows to 4in (10cm) measured over st st on 6½mm/No 3 needles.

Body (make 1)
Using beige, cast on 16 sts.
* Working in st st, work as follows:
Next row (wrong side): P.
Next row: Inc knitwise in every st * – 32 sts.
Rep from * to * once more – 64 sts.
Work straight until body measures 7in (18cm), ending p row.
** **Next row:** (K2 tog) to end.
Next row: P ** – 32 sts.
Rep from ** to ** once more – 16 sts.
Cast off.

Head (make 1)
Using beige, cast on 12 sts.
Work as given for body from * to * until there are 48 sts.
Work 17 rows straight, so ending p row.
Work as given for body from ** to ** until there are 6 sts.
Run a thread through rem sts.

Muzzle (make 1)
Using cream, cast on 36 sts.
Beg k row and working in st st, work 6 rows.
Work as given for body from ** to ** until 9 sts rem.
Run a thread through rem sts.

Arms (make 2)
Using beige, cast on 2 sts.
Beg k row and working in st st, inc 1 st each end of first, then every foll alt row until there are 28 sts.
Work 2½in (6cm) straight, ending p row.
Work as given for body from ** to ** until there are 7 sts.
Run a thread through rem sts.

Legs (make 2)
Using cream, cast on 7 sts.
Work as given for body from * to * until there are 28 sts.
Work 1 row.
Next row: K10, inc knitwise in next 8 sts, k10 – 36 sts.
Next row: P.
Next row: K14, inc knitwise in next 8 sts, k14 – 44 sts.
Next row: P.
Change to beige and work 4 rows.
Next row: K14, (k2 tog) 8 times, k14 – 36 sts.
Next row: P.
Next row: K10, (k2 tog) 8 times, k10 – 28 sts.
Work a further 2½in (6cm) straight.
Cast off loosely.

Tummy patch (make 1)
Using cream, cast on 6 sts.
Beg k row and working in st st, inc 1 st each end of next 3 rows, then every foll alt row until there are 16 sts.
Work 10 rows straight.
Dec 1 st each end of next and foll alt row.
Work 1 row.
Dec 1 st each end of every row until there are 6 sts.
Cast off.

Ears (make 2)
Using beige, cast on 10 sts.
*** Beg k row and working in st st, work 8 rows.
Dec 1 st each end of next 2 rows.
Cast off ***.

Ear linings (make 2)
Using cream, cast on 8 sts.
Work as given for ears from *** to ***.

Front paw patches (make 2)
Using cream, work as given for ear linings.

Finishing
Join body seam and fill. Join head seam, insert toy safety eyes, fill and attach. Join sides of muzzle, fill and attach open ended by cast on edge to front of head. Join leg seams matching colours, fill and attach open ended. Join arm seams, leaving complete increased top edge open, fill and attach by this edge. Sew on tummy and paw patches. Line ears and attach with bases curved to give shape. Embroider nose and mouth and add bow.

Panda bear

Pandas have become a symbol for nature lovers everywhere. Make your own panda to show that you care too. This one is looking for someone to love – it could be you.

Materials
1 (50g) ball Sirdar Country Style Double Knitting in each of black and white; pair of 4mm/No 8 knitting needles; 1 pair toy safety eyes; 1 toy safety nose; washable polyester toy filling.

Measurements
Approx 9in (25cm) tall when seated.

Tension
24 sts and 30 rows to 4in (10cm) measured over st st on 4mm/No 8 knitting needles.
Note: Work as given for Traditional teddy bear on page 36, but in the colours given here. Because a finer yarn on smaller needles is used, the pieces will be smaller, and they are made up differently to create the characteristic panda shape.

Body White.
Head White.
Arms Black.
Legs and feet Black, but work only 2in (5cm) straight after the foot shaping.
Muzzle White, but work only 1in (2.5cm) before shaping.
Ears Black.

Eye patches (make 2)
Using black, cast on 4 sts.
Beg k row and working in st st, inc 1 st each end of next row – 6 sts.
Work 4 rows.
Dec 1 st each end of next row – 4 sts.
Inc 1 st each end of next 2 rows – 8 sts.
Work 6 rows.
Dec 1 st each end of next row – 6 sts.
Cast off.

Finishing
Join body seam and fill. Join head seam and before filling, attach eye patches symmetrically to the front of the head with the smaller part of the eye patch towards the top with the patches sloping characteristically outwards to cover the cheeks, insert toy safety eyes centrally into the top part of each eye patch. Fill and close head and attach. Join sides of muzzle, insert toy safety nose, fill and attach open ended to front of head by cast on edge. Join arm seams, fill lightly and attach with top of arm flattened to shoulder to give characteristic panda shape. Join leg seams, fill and attach in a similar way to sides of bottom of body. Double ears, join edges and attach with bases slightly curved.

Embroider nose and mouth in straight stitches (above) for teddy bears. Work stitches as below for small animals

Polar bear

You may not see polar bears very often now, unless you are lucky enough to visit the Arctic. They are not very happy in zoos, but this knitted one will be delighted to come and live in any child's bedroom.

Materials
1 (100g) ball Sirdar Country Style Chunky in white; pair of 6½mm/No 3 knitting needles; 1 pair toy safety eyes; 1 toy safety nose; washable polyester toy filling.

Measurements
Approx 7in (18cm) tall.

Tension
14 sts and 19 rows to 4in (10cm) measured over st st on 6½mm/No 3 needles.

Main body and head (make 1)
Cast on 6 sts and mark centre of row.
Working in st st, work as follows:
* Next row (wrong side): P.
Next row: Inc knitwise in first st, k to 1 st before centre, inc knitwise in next 2 sts, k to last st, inc knitwise in last st.
Next row: P.
Next row: Inc knitwise in first st, k to last st, inc knitwise in last st *.
Rep from * to * until there are 48 sts.
Work straight until work measures 13in (33cm) from cast on edge, ending p row.
Next row: (K2 tog) to end.
Next row: P.
Rep these 2 rows until 6 sts rem.
Run a thread through rem sts.

Feet and legs (make 4)
Cast on 5 sts.

Working in st st, work as follows:
Next row (wrong side): P.
Next row: Inc knitwise in every st – 10 sts.
Rep the last 2 rows once more – 20 sts.
Next row: P.
Next row: K7, inc knitwise in next 6 sts, k7 – 26 sts.
Work 5 rows.
Next row: K7, (k2 tog) 6 times, k7 – 20 sts.
Work 8 rows straight.
Cast off loosely.

Ears (make 2)
Cast on 4 sts.
Beg k row and working in st st, work 3 rows.
Next row: P2 tog, p2 tog tbl – 2 sts.
Next row: Inc knitwise in each st – 4 sts.
Work 3 rows.
Cast off.

Tail (make 1)
Cast on 4 sts.
Beg k row and working in st st, work 4 rows.
Next row: (Work 2 tog) twice – 2 sts.
Work 2 tog, fasten off.

Finishing
Join body and head seam leaving an opening, insert safety toy eyes and nose, fill and close opening. Join leg seams, fill and attach open ended. Double ears and attach. Attach tail.

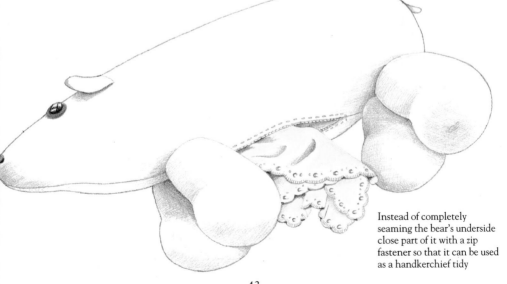

Instead of completely seaming the bear's underside close part of it with a zip fastener so that it can be used as a handkerchief tidy

Teddy bears picnic

Teddy bears picnic

Four bears were invited to this picnic, all in different colours. You can make as many bears as you like. If you then need a bigger rug, simply cast on more stitches and repeat the stripe pattern until the rug is the size required. The bears would make wonderful stocking fillers.

Materials
Sirdar Country Style Double Knitting: **For each bear:** Small quantity of any brown; oddments of Double Knitting for embroidery; pair of 4mm/No 8 knitting needles; washable polyester toy filling; ribbon; **Rug:** Small quantities of dark green, red, navy and white.

Measurements
Each bear is approx 2½in (6cm) tall when sitting.
The rug is approximately 10×12in (25×30cm).

Tension
24 sts and 30 rows to 4in (10cm) measured over st st on 4mm/No 8 needles.

Bear
Body and head (make 1)
Cast on 5 sts.
Working in st st, work as follows:
* **Next row (wrong side):** P.
Next row: Inc knitwise in every st* – 10 sts.
Rep from * to * once more – 20 sts.
Work 9 rows straight, so ending p row.
** **Next row:** (K2 tog) to end.
Next row: P ** – 10 sts.
Next row: K.
Rep from * to * once – 20 sts.
Work 5 rows straight, so ending p row.
Rep from ** to ** twice – 5 sts.
Run a thread through rem sts.

Legs (make 2)
Cast on 10 sts.
*** Beg k row and working in st st, work 8 rows.
Next row: (K2 tog) to end – 5 sts.
Run a thread through rem sts ***.

Arms (make 2)
Cast on 2 sts.
Beg k row and working in st st, in 1 st each end of first, then every foll alt row until there are 10 sts.
Next row: P.
Work as given for legs from *** to ***.

Ears (make 2)
Cast on 4 sts.
Next row: K.
Next row: P.
Next row: K2 tog, k2 tog tbl – 2 sts.
Next row: Inc purlwise in each st – 4 sts.
Next row: K.
Next row: P.
Cast off.

Finishing
Join body and head seam leaving an opening, fill, close opening. Join arm and leg seams, fill and attach open ended. Double ears, join edges and attach. Embroider features and tie ribbon bow around neck.

Rug
Using dark green, cast on 72 sts.
Beg k row and working in st st, work in the following stripe pattern: 3 rows dark green, 2 rows red, 2 rows navy, 1 row white, 4 rows dark green, 1 row red, 3 rows dark green.
Rep these 16 rows 4 times more – 80 rows in all.
Cast off loosely in dark green.

Finishing
Using navy, red and white, embroider vertical lines in a repeating pattern, creating a tartan effect.

3: CHRISTMAS FUN

Christmas mobile

This mobile for a child's room has five small figures suspended from ring: two elves, two fairies and an angel. The characters are made from the basic pattern for the small figures on page 18, with additions and variations as given.*

Materials
Sirdar Double Knitting in assorted colours as chosen or as stated in the pattern; oddments of yarn for embroidery; assorted trims; pair of 4mm/No 8 knitting needles; craft ring approx 8in (20cm) diameter; length of Christmas ribbon; nylon invisible line (such as fishing line or strong nylon thread); washable polyester toy filling.

Tension
24 sts and 30 rows to 4in (10cm) measured over st st on 4mm/No 8 needles.

ELVES

Make 2 complete elves using small figure basic pattern on page 18.

Main piece

Using bright green, cast on each leg and work inc rows and first 2 straight rows, change to red and work 8 rows, complete legs, body and first 4 rows of neck shaping in bright green, then complete in peach.

Arms

Using bright green, cast on and work inc rows and first 5 rows straight, then complete in peach.

Hat (make 1)

Using red, cast on 18 sts.
Beg k row and working in st st, dec 1 st each end of 3rd, then every row to 2 sts.
Work 2 tog and fasten off.

Finishing

Join seam and sew on hat. Embroider features. Sew on a red ribbon belt and embroider a buckle.

FAIRIES

Make 2 complete fairies using small figures pattern on page 18, one with pink clothes, the other with pale blue clothes.

Main piece

Using peach, cast on and work both legs. Work body and first 4 rows of neck shaping in either pink or pale blue then complete in peach.

Arms

In peach throughout.

Skirt (make 1)

Using pink or pale blue, cast on 72 sts and k 4 rows.
Beg k row, work in st st until skirt measures 1½in (4cm) from cast on edge, ending p row.
Next row: (K2 tog) to end – 36 sts.
Cast off.

Finishing

Join skirt seam. Gather cast off edge and attach around waist. Add pink or pale blue hair and embroider features. Cut two squares of net, place one on top of the other and run a gather thread down the centre, pull tight to form a bow or wings shape, attach to centre of back.

ANGEL

Make Angel using small figures pattern on page 18.

Main piece

Using peach, cast on and work both legs, change to white and work body and first 4 rows of neck shaping, then complete in peach.

Arms

Using white, cast on and work inc rows and first 8 rows straight, then complete in peach.

Skirt (make 1)

Using white, cast on 72 sts and k 4 rows.
Beg k row, work in st st until skirt measures 3in (8cm) from cast on edge, ending p row.
Next row: (K2 tog) to end – 36 sts.
Cast off.

Wings (make 2)

Using bright yellow, cast on 2 sts.
Working in garter st (k every row), inc 1 st each end of 3rd, then every foll 8th row to 10 sts.
Dec 1 st each end of every foll alt row to 2 sts.
Work 2 tog, fasten off.

Finishing

Join skirt seam. Gather cast off edge and attach around waist. Attach a wing to each shoulder with the cast on edge as the bottom point. Add long yellow hair, caught down with a circle of gold thread. Embroider features. With gold thread, embroider around bottom of skirt and around waist.

Finishing mobile

Using nylon line, attach the figures around the craft ring, arranging them at different heights. Cut 3 equal lengths of Christmas ribbon and tie to the ring. Knot ribbon ends together. A brass ring can be added for hanging. Decorate mobile with bows.

Reindeer

This Christmas reindeer toy is straight from Lapland. His name is, of course, Rudolf – you can tell by his red nose!

Materials
1 (50g) ball Sirdar Country Style Double Knitting in beige, small quantity in black, brown and red; oddments of yarn for embroidery; pair of 4mm/No 8 knitting needles; washable polyester toy filling.
Measurement
Approx 12in (30cm) tall.
Tension
24 sts and 30 rows to 4in (10cm) measured over st st on 4mm/No 8 needles.

Body (make 1)
Using beige, cast on 5 sts.
* Working in st st, work as follows:
Next row (wrong side): P.
Next row: Inc knitwise in every st * – 10 sts.
Rep from * to * until there are 80 sts.
Work a further 7in (18cm) straight, ending p row.
** **Next row:** (K2 tog) to end.
Next row: P ** – 40 sts.
Rep from ** to ** until 5 sts rem.
Run a thread through rem sts.

Head (make 1)
Using brown, cast on 5 sts.
Work as given for body from * to * until there are 40 sts.
Work 7 rows straight.
Change to beige and work a further 20 rows, so ending p row.
Work as given for body from ** to ** until 5 sts rem.
Run a thread through rem sts.

Neck (make 1)
Using beige, cast on 36 sts.
Beg k row, work 14 rows in st st.
Cast off loosely.

Legs (make 4)
Using beige, cast on 20 sts.

Beg k row and working in st st, work 18 rows.
Change to brown and work 6 rows.
Change to black and work 2 rows, then work as given for body from ** to ** until 5 sts rem.
Run a thread through rem sts.

Tail (make 1)
Using brown, cast on 8 sts.
Beg k row and working in st st, dec 1 st each end of every 3rd row until 2 sts rem.
Change to beige and inc 1 st each end of next, then every 3rd row until there are 8 sts.
Work 2 rows.
Cast off.

Ears (make 2)
Using beige, cast on 10 sts.
Beg k row and working in st st, work 8 rows.
Dec 1 st each end of next 2 rows – 6 sts.
Change to brown and inc 1 st each end of next 2 rows – 10 sts.
Work 8 rows.
Cast off.

Nose (make 1)
Using red, cast on 6 sts and work as given for body from * to * once – 12 sts.
Work 7 rows straight.
Next row: (K2 tog) to end – 6 sts.
Run a thread through rem sts.

Antler stems (make 2)
Using brown, cast on 10 sts.
Beg k row and working in st st, work 16 rows straight, ending p row.
Next row: (K2 tog) to end – 5 sts.
Run a thread through rem sts.

Antler lower branches (make 2)
Using brown, work as for antler stems, but work only 10 rows straight.

Antler upper branches (make 2)
Using brown, work as for antler stems, but work only 6 rows straight.

Finishing
Join body seam leaving an opening, fill, close opening. Join leg seams matching colours, fill and attach with ends flat. Join side edges of neck to form a cylinder and attach to body by cast on edge, fill neck. Join head seam matching colours, fill before completing seam and attach to top of neck with brown end towards the front. Fill and attach nose. Double ears, join edges and attach with bases doubled. Seam and fill antler branches and stems. Attach stems to head and branches to stems. Double tail, seam and attach. Embroider features (see picture).

Tree trims

This basic pattern is for making a small bauble and those pictured are worked in stripes, decorated with ribbon. They can, of course, be made in any yarns and decorated with sequins, beads, tinsel – anything you like. The baubles would be especially nice knitted in gold or silver yarn.

Materials
Sirdar Double Knitting, small quantities of 3 contrast colours; pair of 4mm/No 8 knitting needles; oddments of gold and silver thread; ribbon scraps for decoration; washable polyester toy filling.

Measurement
Approx 2½in (6cm) in diameter.

Tension
24 sts and 30 rows to 4in (10cm) measured over st st on 4mm/No 8 needles.

Special Note: These baubles are too small to be given to babies and very young children to play with. Use as decorations only and hang on the tree out of their reach.

Basic pattern
Using first colour, cast on 5 sts.
Working in st st, work as follows:
Next row (wrong side): P.
Next row: Inc knitwise in every st – 10 sts.
Rep these 2 rows until there are 40 sts.
Work a further 4 rows.
Change to 2nd colour and work 5 rows.
Change to 3rd colour and work 4 rows, so ending p row.
Next row: (K2 tog) to end – 20 sts.
Next row: P.
Rep these 2 rows until 5 sts rem.
Break off yarn leaving a long end, thread end through rem sts, then join row ends leaving an opening, fill, close. Decorate with ribbon, adding a silver thread tassel and hanging loop.

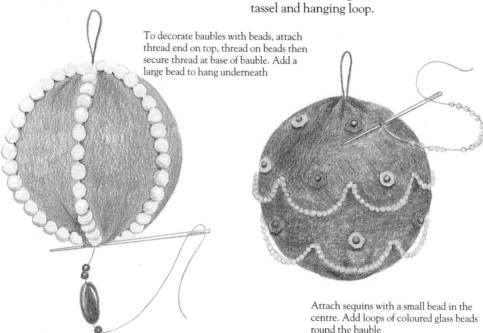

To decorate baubles with beads, attach thread end on top, thread on beads then secure thread at base of bauble. Add a large bead to hang underneath

Attach sequins with a small bead in the centre. Add loops of coloured glass beads round the bauble

Father Christmas

Father Christmas makes a lovely gift or a table decoration. This could be an original way to present a gift if it were small enough to be wrapped inside the sack. For a party, fill the sack with sweets or small gifts. Father Christmas is worked from the basic pattern for large dolls on page 28, with the variations and additions below.

Materials
1 (50g) ball Sirdar Country Style Double Knitting in dark red; small quantities of Double Knitting in black, green, white, brown and beige; oddments of yarn for embroidery; pair of 4mm/No 8 knitting needles; washable polyester toy filling.

Measurements
Approx 12in (30cm) tall.

Tension
24 sts and 30 rows to 4in (10cm) measured over st st on 4mm/No 8 needles.

Main body and legs
(Worked from the large dolls pattern on page 28 in colours as stated.) Using black, cast on each leg and work foot and first 1½in (4cm) of leg. Work 4 rows white, complete legs and body in dark red.

Arms
Using dark red, cast on and work all inc rows and work 2in (6cm) straight, complete in beige.

Head
Work in beige throughout.

Jacket
Main piece (make 1)
Using white, cast on 78 sts.
Beg k row and working in st st, work 6 rows, change to red and cont until jacket measures 4in (10cm) from cast on edge, ending p row.
Next row: (K1, k2 tog) to end – 52 sts.
Work 7 rows, so ending p row.
Divide for armholes:
Next row: K13, turn, leaving rem sts on a holder, p to end.
Work 6 rows, so ending at outside (front neck) edge.
Next row: Cast off 7, k6.
Work 5 rows.
Cast off.
Rejoin yarn to inside edge of rem sts, k26, turn, leaving rem sts on a holder, p to end.
Work 12 rows.
Cast off.
Rejoin yarn to inside edge of rem sts and work 9 rows, so ending at outside (front neck) edge.
Next row: Cast off 7, p6.

Work 4 rows.
Cast off.

Sleeves (make 2)
Using white, cast on 30 sts.
Beg k row and working in st st, work 6 rows.
Change to red and work until sleeve measures 3¼in (8cm) from cast on edge.
Cast off loosely.

Hood (make 1)
Using white, cast on 40 sts.
Beg k row and working in st st, work 6 rows.
Change to red and work until hood measures 3¼in (8cm) from cast on edge.
Cast off.

Front borders (both alike)
With right side facing, pick up and k36 sts evenly down the front edge from neck opening, ending half way down the white border.
Beg p row, work 5 rows in st st.
Cast off.

Belt (make 1)
Using brown, cast on 48 sts.
Beg k row and working in st st, work 3 rows.
Cast off loosely.

Sack (make 1)
Using green, cast on 36 sts.
Beg k row, work in st st until sack measures 6in (15cm).
K 4 rows.
Cast off.

Finishing
Make up doll as given on page 30. Join shoulder and sleeve seams of jacket, then sew in sleeves. Double hood and join cast off edge to form back seam. Turn all white edgings to right side and loosely slip st in place. Mark a point ¾in (2cm) away from the front edge at each side of the front neck. Attach hood evenly between these points to the remainder of the neck opening. Join ends of belt together and embroider a buckle. Embroider hair, whiskers and eyebrows in white. Embroider features (see picture). Join bottom and side seam of sack. Thread with a drawstring to close.

Snowman

This snowman is very easy to make, for a toy, a Christmas decoration or for a table centre for a child's party. Adapt the colours of the scarf and hat to suit your own ideas.

Materials
1 (50g) ball Sirdar Country Style Double Knitting in white; small quantities of Double Knitting in royal blue, black, yellow and orange; pair each 3¾mm/No 9 and 4mm/No 8 knitting needles; washable polyester toy filling.

Measurement
Approx 12in (30cm) tall.

Tension
24 sts and 30 rows to 4in (10cm) measured over st st on 4mm/No 8 needles.

Main piece (make 1)
Using 4mm needles and white, cast on 9 sts.
* Working in st st, work as follows:
Next row (wrong side): P.
Next row: Inc knitwise in every st * – 18 sts.
Rep the last 2 rows until there are 72 sts.
Work 8in (20cm) straight, ending p row.
** **Next row:** (K2 tog) to end.
Next row: P ** – 36 sts.
Rep the last 2 rows until 9 sts rem. Run a thread through rem sts.

Head (make 1)
Using 4mm needles and white, cast on 6 sts.
Work as given for main piece from * to * until there are 48 sts.
Work 3in (8cm) straight, ending p row.
Work as given for main piece from ** to ** until 6 sts rem.
Run a thread through rem sts.

Hat
Using 3¾mm needles and blue, cast on 48 sts.
Work 4 rows in k1, p1 rib.
Change to 4mm needles. Beg k row and working in st st, work 2 rows.
Change to yellow and work 4 rows.

Change to blue and work 2 rows, so ending p row.
Work as given for main piece from ** to ** until 6 sts rem. Run a thread through rem sts.

Scarf
Using 3¾mm needles and blue, cast on 13 sts.
Rib row 1: K2, (p1, k1) to last st, k1.
Rib row 2: K1, (p1, k1) to end.
Rep these 2 rows 3 more times.
*** Change to yellow and k 1 row.
Beg rib row 2, work 3 rows in rib.
Change to blue and k 1 row ***.
Beg rib row 2, cont in rib until scarf measures 16in (41cm) from cast on edge, ending rib row 2.
Rep from *** to ***.
Beg rib row 2, work 7 rows in rib.
Cast off in rib.

Pieces of coal (make 5)
Using 4mm needles and black, cast on 1 st and k 3 times into st.
Next row: P.
Next row: K.
P3 tog, fasten off.

Carrot for nose
Using 4mm needles and orange, cast on 9 sts.
Beg k row and working in st st, dec 1 st each end of 3rd, then every foll alt row until 3 sts rem.
Work 2 rows.
Work 3 tog, fasten off.

Finishing
Join body seam, fill. Join head seam, fill, then attach to body. Join hat seam, matching stripes and add a small pompom.

Sew tassels to ends of scarf. Join carrot nose seam, fill and attach open ended. Sew on coal eyes and coat buttons.

The snowman could be made larger by using thicker yarn and larger needles.

4: TOYS AND ANIMALS

Noah and the Ark

The pattern is for the Ark, Mr and Mrs Noah and a selection of animals. Most of the animals are based on the same pattern, worked in different colours and stitched together in different ways. You can use your imagination to turn the same pattern into almost any animal you wish. Mr and Mrs Noah are based on the pattern for the small figures on page 18, with changes to yarn colours and clothing.

Materials
Balls (50g) Sirdar Country Style Double Knitting as follows:
Ark: 4 in dark brown, 1 in pale brown; small quantities of mid-brown; oddments of yarn for embroidery; pair of 4mm/No 8 knitting needles; piece of card 3×9in (8×23cm); washable polyester toy filling.

Figures and animals: Small quantities of contrast colours as stated in the pattern for each variation, oddments of yarn for embroidery; pair of 4mm/No 8 knitting needles; washable polyester toy filling; assorted trims.

Measurements
Ark approx 20in (51cm) long.
Mr and Mrs Noah approx 5in (13cm) tall.
Animals approx 5in (13cm) long (varying heights).

Tension
24 sts and 30 rows to 4in (10cm) measured over st st on 4mm/No 8 needles.

ARK
Ark side (make 2)
Using dark brown, cast on 84 sts.
Beg k row and work in st st, work in stripe pattern: 6 rows dark brown, 2 rows light brown and 8 rows dark brown, then repeat the last 10 rows throughout: **at the same time,** inc 1 st each end of every 3rd row until there are 120 sts.
With dark brown, work 2 rows straight, so ending with an 8-row dark brown stripe and p row.
Next row: P.
Beg p row and working in st st with dark brown, dec 1 st each end of every 3rd row until there are 84 sts.
Work 2 rows.
Cast off loosely.

Deck (make 1)
Using dark brown, cast on 60 sts.
Beg k row and working in st st, inc 1 st each end of every row until there are 108 sts.
Dec 1 st each end of every row until there are 60 sts.
Cast off loosely.

Deck house side walls and roof (make 1)
Using mid-brown, cast on 42 sts.
Beg k row and working in st st, work in stripes of 4 rows mid-brown and 2 rows dark brown until wall measures approx 5in (13cm), ending with a mid-brown stripe and p row.
Change to pale brown and tile pattern:
Next row: K.
Next row: K.
Next row: (K1, p1) to end.
Next row: (K1, p1) to end.
Rep these 4 rows until tile pattern measures approx 7in (18cm), ending with 2nd K row.

Change to mid-brown. Beg k row and working in st st, work in stripe pattern and length to match first side wall.
Cast off loosely.

Deck house end walls (make 2)
Using mid-brown, cast on 24 sts.
Beg k row and working in st st, work in stripes of 4 rows mid-brown and 2 rows dark brown until wall measures approx 5in (13cm), ending with a mid-brown stripe and p row when pattern matches side walls.
Keeping stripe pattern correct, dec 1 st each end of next, then every foll alt row until 2 sts rem.
Work 2 tog, fasten off.

Deck house door (make 1)
Using black, cast on 10 sts.
Beg k row and working in st st, work 18 rows.
Dec 1 st each end of the next 2 alt rows – 6 sts.
Cast off.

Gangway (make 1)
Using mid-brown, cast on 32 sts.
Next row: K.
Next row: P.
Next row: K8, p16, k8.
Next row: P.
Next row: K.
Next row: P.
Rep these 6 rows until work measures 9in (23cm), ending p row.
Cast off.

Finishing
Fold each side along wrong side row and join together. Join the two sides by their ends and bottom edges to form the boat shape matching stripes. Fill and insert deck evenly approx ¾in (2cm) below the top of the sides.
Sew in ends of deck house matching stripes and matching roof tiles to shaped tops of deck house ends. Fill and attach to centre of deck. Sew door centrally to one end. Join sides of gangway and insert card, so that this seam is at the centre of the back. Close ends (see illustration).

MR NOAH
Using the small figures basic pattern on page 18, work as follows:

Main piece
Using dark brown, cast on and work inc rows and first 2 rows straight of each leg, change to pale brown and complete legs. Work body and first 4 rows of neck shaping in grey, complete in pale brown.

Arms
Using grey, cast on and work inc rows and first 9 rows straight, complete in pale brown.

Robe halves (make 2)
Using grey, cast on 24 sts.

Fold side piece on purl row, join on sides and bottom edge

Sew two side pieces together to make the hull

Stuff the hull, then sew in the deck

K 4 rows.
Beg k row and working in st st, work until robe measures 3½in (9cm) from cast on edge, ending p row.
Next row: (K2 tog) to end – 12 sts. Cast off.

Cloak (make 1)
Using dark red, cast on 36 sts.
K 4 rows.
Beg k row and working in st st, work until cloak measures 4in (10cm) from cast on edge, ending p row.
Next row: (K3 tog) to end – 12 sts. Cast off.

Finishing
Make up as given for small figures basic pattern on page 19. Join sides of robe and catch shoulders together, leaving a 1¼in (3cm) armhole. Attach cloak to shoulders of robe. Sew on long white hair and a white beard and moustache. Make cords with dark red to tie around waist and hair. Embroider features (see picture).

MRS NOAH

Using the small figures basic pattern on page 18, work as follows:

Main piece

Using mid-brown, cast on and work inc rows and first 2 rows straight, change to pale peach and complete legs. Work body and first 4 rows of neck shaping in pale blue, complete in pale peach.

Arms

Using pale blue, cast on and work inc rows and first 9 rows straight, complete in pale peach.

Skirt (make 1)

Using pale blue, cast on 48 sts.
* K 4 rows.
Beg k row and working in st st, work until skirt measures 2½in (6cm) from cast on edge, ending p row.
Next row: (K2 tog) to end.
Cast off *.

Apron (make 1)

Using white, cast on 12 sts and work as given for skirt from * to *, but work to a total of only 1½in (4cm) straight before shaping.

Finishing

Make up figure as given for small figures basic pattern on page 19. Join skirt. Gather cast off edge and attach around waist. Attach lengths of white yarn to top corners of apron and tie around waist with a bow. Sew on grey hair and style into a bun. Embroider features (see picture).

BASIC ANIMAL PATTERN
(makes 1 animal)

Body (make 1)

Cast on 6 sts.
* Working in st st, work as follows:
Next row (wrong side): P.
Next row: Inc knitwise in every st * – 12 sts.
Rep from * to * once more – 24 sts.
Work 15 rows straight, so ending p row.

** Next row: (K2 tog) to end.
Next row: P ** – 12 sts.
Rep from ** to ** once more – 6 sts.
Run a thread through rem sts, use to seam, then fill.

Head (make 1)

Cast on 6 sts and work as given for body from * to * once – 12 sts.
Work 7 rows straight, so ending p row.
Work as given for body from ** to ** once – 6 sts.
Run a thread through rem sts, use to seam, then fill.

Legs (make 4)

Cast on 5 sts and work as given for body from * to * once – 10 sts.
Work 7 rows straight.
Cast off loosely. Seam, leaving cast off edge open and fill.

Neck (make 1)

Cast on 10 sts.
Beg k row and working in st st, work 4 rows.
Cast off loosely. Seam side edges, forming a tube and fill leaving both ends open.

Ears (make 2)

Cast on 4 sts.
Next row: K.
Next row: P.
Next row: (K2 tog) twice – 2 sts.
P2 tog, fasten off.

Tail

Cast on 6 sts. Cast off.

VARIATIONS
(make 2 of each creature)

Lions

Work as given for basic pattern in pale brown throughout, omitting neck and ears. Attach legs so that animal stands. Attach head and tail. On one lion, sew a dark brown mane.
Embroider features (see picture) and attach a small dark brown tassel to end of tail. Add large French knots either side of head as ears.

Zebras

Work as given for basic pattern, working body, head, legs and neck in stripes of 2 rows black and 2 rows white throughout. Ears in black. Tail in white. Sew on legs so that animal stands. Attach neck and head. Sew on tail and add a black tassel to end. Stitch on a short white mane. Double cast on edge of ears and attach. Embroider eyes (see picture).

Giraffes

Work as given for basic pattern in yellow, but work 15 rows straight on legs and 12 rows on neck before casting off. Attach legs so that animal stands. Attach neck and head. Sew on tail. Embroider body and neck with brown spots. Embroider features (see picture) and sew on two short lengths of brown yarn as horns. Double cast on edge of ears and attach.

Monkeys

Work as given for basic pattern in dark brown, omitting neck and ears. Cast on 12 sts for tail.

Muzzle (make 1)

With peach cast on 1 st and work 4 times knitwise into this st.

Next row: P.

Next row: K.

Next row: (P2 tog) twice.

K2 tog, fasten off.

Attach two legs, flat ended, to one end of body and the other two flat ended to shoulders to form arms. Attach tail, head and muzzle.

Embroider features (see picture). Work large French knots in peach yarn on either side of head as ears.

Doves

Body (make 1 for each dove)

Do not use basic pattern but work as follows:
Using white, cast on 2 sts.
Working in st st, work as follows:
Next row (wrong side): P.
Next row: Work 3 times knitwise into each st – 6 sts.
Next row: P.
Next row: (Inc knitwise in next st, k1, inc knitwise in next st) twice – 10 sts.
Work 5 rows.
Next row: (K2 tog) to end – 5 sts.

Run a thread through rem sts.
Join seam and fill.

Head (make 1 for each dove)

Using white, cast on 1 st and work 4 times knitwise into this st.
Work 3 rows in st st.
Next row: (K2 tog) twice – 2 sts.
P2 tog, fasten off.
Join seam, fill and attach to body. Embroider a wing line on each side and embroider eyes. Add a single, short length of pink yarn as a beak.

Mice

Do not use basic pattern but work as follows:
Using grey, work 1 body for each mouse as
given for dove's body. Using pink, sew on a
tail, embroider a nose and French knot ears.
Embroider eyes in black.

Crocodiles

Back (make 1 for each crocodile)

Do not use basic pattern but work as follows:
Using dark green, cast on 1 st and work 3
times knitwise into this st.
Work in moss st as follows:
Next row: K1, p1, k1.
Rep this row 3 more times.
Next row: Inc knitwise in first st, p1, inc
knitwise in last st – 5 sts.
Next row: (P1, k1) to last st, p1.
Rep this row 3 more times.
Next row: Inc purlwise in first st, k1, p1, k1,
inc purlwise in last st – 7 sts.
Next row: (K1, p1) 3 times, k1.

Rep this row 3 times.
Next row: Inc knitwise in first st, (p1, k1)
twice, p1, inc knitwise in last st – 9 sts.
Next row: P1, (k1, p1) to end.
Rep the last row until work measures 5in
(13cm) from the cast on st.
Keeping moss st pattern correct, dec 1 st
each end of next, then every foll 4th row to
5 sts.
Work 3 rows.
Cast off.

Belly (make 1 for each crocodile)

Using light brown, cast on 1 st and work 3
times knitwise into this st.
Beg p row and working in st st, inc 1 st each
end of 4th, then every foll 5th row to 9 sts.
Work straight until belly measures 5in
(13cm) from cast on st.
Dec 1 st each end of next, then every foll
4th row to 5 sts.
Work 3 rows.
Cast off.

Mouth lining (make 1 for each crocodile)
Using pale peach, cast on 5 sts.
Beg k row and working in st st, work 3 rows.
Inc 1 st each end of next, then every foll 4th
row to 9 sts.
Dec 1 st each end of every foll 4th row until
5 sts rem.
Work 3 rows.
Cast off.

Feet (make 4 for each crocodile)
Using dark green, cast on 1 st and work 4

times knitwise into this st.
Next row: P.
Next row: Inc knitwise in every st – 8 sts.
Beg p row, work 4 rows straight in st st.
Cast off.

Finishing
Double mouth lining and sew to shaped sides
of head end (cast off end) of back and belly.
Join sides of back to belly and fill. Double
feet and attach. Embroider eyes (see picture).

73

On the road

All children love vehicles, and these are safe enough for the smallest child. Make lots in bright colours and they will give pleasure for many hours. There are three basic shapes, a car, a van and a pick-up.

Materials
Sirdar Double Knitting, small quantity in contrast colours and black for each vehicle; pair of 4mm/No 8 knitting needles; washable polyster toy filling.
Tension
24 sts and 30 rows to 4in (10cm) measured over st st on 4mm/No 8 needles.

CAR

Left side of car body (make 1)
* Using black, cast on 36 sts.
Beg k row and working in st st, work 2 rows.
Change to chosen vehicle colour and work 8 rows, so ending p row.
Dec 1 st each end of next 2 rows* – 32 sts.
Shape back: Cast off 6 sts at beg of next row – 26 sts.
Shape front: Cast off 10 sts at beg of next row – 16 sts.
** Dec 1 st each end of every foll 3rd row until 10 sts rem.
Cast off **.

Right side of car body (make 1)
Work as given for left side of car body from * to *.
Shape front: Cast off 10 sts at beg of next row – 22 sts.
Shape back: Cast off 6 sts at beg of next row – 16 sts.
Work as for left side of body from ** to **.

Centre strip of car (make 1)
Using black, cast on 15 sts.
Beg k row and working in st st, work 45 rows, so ending k row.
Next row: K.
Beg k row and working in st st, work 2 rows.
Change to chosen vehicle colour.
Beg k row and working in st st, work 70 rows, so ending p row.
Change to black and work 2 rows.
Cast off loosely.

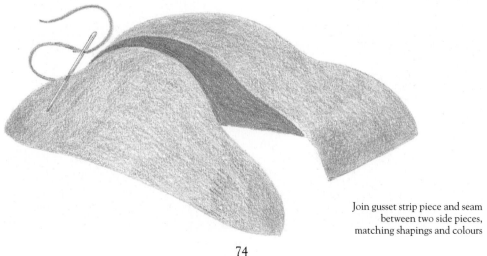

Join gusset strip piece and seam
between two side pieces,
matching shapings and colours

VAN

Left side of van body
Work as for left side of car body from * to *.
Work 1 row.
Shape front: Cast off 10 sts at beg of next
row − 22 sts.
*** Dec 1 st at front edge only on every foll
3rd row until 19 sts rem.
Cast off ***.

Right side of van body
Work as for left side of car body from * to *.
Shape front: Cast off 10 sts at beg of next
row − 22 sts.
Work as for left side of van body from *** to
***.

Centre strip of van
Work as given for centre strip of car.

PICK-UP

Left side of pick-up body
Work as for left side of car body from * to *.
Shape back: Cast off 12 sts at beg of next
row − 20 sts.
Shape front: Cast off 10 sts at beg of next
row − 10 sts.
**** Dec 1 st at front edge only on every foll
3rd row until 7 sts rem.
Cast off ****.

Right side of pick-up body
Work as given for left side of car body from *
to *.
Shape front: Cast off 10 sts at beg of next
row − 22 sts.
Shape back: Cast off 12 sts at beg of next
row − 10 sts.
Work as for left side of pick-up body from
**** to ****.

Centre strip of pick-up
Work as given for centre strip of car.

Finishing
Join cast on and cast off edges of centre strip
together. Sew in sides so that colours and
shapings match on either side of the centre
strip, leaving an opening, fill, then close
opening.
Embroider simple shapes for wheels, windows
and lights (see picture and illustration).

Colourful balls

This simple pattern makes a segmented ball. Two sizes in any combination of colours can be made. The small ball is knitted in pastel colours for a baby's pram toy and the larger is worked in bright colours for older children.

Materials
Sirdar Double Knitting, 25(75)g in contrast colours; pair of 4mm/No 8 knitting needles; washable polyester toy filling.
Measurements
Approx 5[8]in (13[20]cm) in diameter.
Tension
24 sts and 30 rows to 4in (10cm) measured over st st on 4mm/No 8 needles.
Note: Instructions are for smaller ball with the larger size in brackets [ ].

BASIC PATTERN

Segment (make 8)
Cast on 1 st.
Next row (right side): Work 4 times knitwise into this stitch.
Beg p row and working in st st, inc 1 st each end of every foll 4th row until there are 12[18] sts.
Work 27[33] rows straight, so ending p row.
Dec 1 st each end of next, then every foll 4th row until 4 sts rem.
Work 3 rows.
Next row: K2 tog, k2 tog tbl.
P2 tog, fasten off.

Finishing
Join row ends of segments together leaving an opening, fill, then join opening.

Soft baby balls are a good way of using up odd scraps of yarn and you can knit up quite short lengths changing colours in the middle of a row. But always try and use yarns of comparable weight so that the tension is the same throughout.

Seam two ball segments together

Join other segments in the same way

Stuff through open seam, then close with oversewing

Tabby cat

This lovable toy can be striped in grey and black, ginger and cream or be knitted a plain colour. The pattern could also be adapted to make a Siamese, a black and white, or even a long-haired breed if knitted in a brushed yarn. The choice is yours.

Materials
Sirdar Wash 'n' Wear Crepe Double Knitting, part balls in beige, brown and grey; oddments of yarn for embroidery; pair of 4mm/No 8 knitting needles; washable polyester toy filling.
Measurement
Approx 10in (25cm) tall.
Tension
24 sts and 30 rows to 4in (10cm) measured over st st on 4mm/No 8 needles.

Base (make 1)
Using beige, cast on 16 sts.
Beg k row and working in st st, inc 1 st each end of every row to 26 sts, then on every alt row to 34 sts.
Work 4 rows straight.
Dec 1 st each end of next, then every alt row until 26 sts rem, then every row until 16 sts rem.
Cast off.

Main body piece (make 1)
Using brown, cast on 78 sts.
Beg k row and working in st st, work in stripes of 4 rows brown and 4 rows grey until work measures 7in (18cm) from cast on edge, ending p row.
Cont in stripe pattern
Shape top:
* Next row: (K2 tog) to end – 39 sts.
Next row: P *.
Next row: K1, (k2 tog) to end – 20 sts.
Next row: P.
Rep from * to * once more – 10 sts.
Run a thread through rem sts.

Bib front (make 1)
Using beige, cast on 15 sts.

Beg k row and working in st st, work 7in (18cm) straight, ending p row.
Dec 1 st each end of every row to 3 sts.
Work 3 tog, fasten off.

Head (make 1)
Using brown, cast on 9 sts.
Working in st st, work as follows:
Next row (wrong side): P.
Next row: Inc knitwise in every st – 18 sts.
Rep these 2 rows once more – 36 sts.
Next row: P.
Change to grey and work 4 rows.
Change to brown and work 4 rows.
Cont in this stripe pattern until 36 rows of stripe pattern have been worked, so completing a grey stripe and ending p row – 9 stripes worked in all.
Cont in brown.
Next row: (K2 tog) to end – 18 sts.
Next row: P.
Rep these 2 rows once more – 9 sts.
Run a thread through rem sts.

Nose (make 1)
Using beige, cast on 6 sts.
Working in st st, work as follows:
Next row (wrong side): P.
Next row: Inc knitwise in every st – 12 sts.
Work 15 rows straight, so ending p row.
Next row: (K2 tog) to end – 6 sts.
Next row: P.
Run a thread through rem sts.

Ears (make 2)
Using brown, cast on 16 sts.
Beg k row and working in st st, dec 1 st each end of first, then every alt row to 2 sts.
Work 2 tog, fasten off.

Stuffed dragon toy

The dragon puppet could also be made into a long, cuddly soft toy by knitting extra length on both the back and belly pieces. But note that you will need extra yarn. If you knit 30 more rows on both pieces, the finished toy will be about 16in (40.5cm) long. When you have completed the puppet toy, as instructed, finish the making up as for the puppet and then stuff lightly along the entire length from the open tail end to the head. To finish the toy, gather the open end with matching yarn. The puppet would also make an unusual and amusing draught excluder

but you would need to knit enough rows to fit the toy across the door. Check the tension information as this will give you a guide to the amount of extra knitting you have to do.

For fun, you might decorate the puppet with glass beads and sequins, to give it more the look of a monster. Embroidery could be added also in bright colours – acid yellow, green, red and blue. If you are planning a puppet show, why not make two dragons, in different colour schemes, so that they can have a battle!

Ear linings (make 2)
Using beige, work as given for ears, but cast on only 14 sts.

Front paws (make 2)
Using brown, cast on 7 sts.
Working in st st, work as follows:
Next row (wrong side): P.
Next row: Inc knitwise in every st – 14 sts.
Rep the last 2 rows once more – 28 sts.
Work 5 rows straight, so ending p row.
** Next row: (K2 tog) to end – 14 sts.
Next row: P.
Rep these 2 rows once more – 7 sts.
Run a thread through rem sts **.

Tail (make 1)
Using brown, cast on 28 sts.
Beg k row, work in st st in stripes of 4 rows brown and 4 rows grey until tail measures

7½in (19cm) from cast on edge, ending p row.
Cont in stripe pattern, work as given for front paws from ** to **.

Finishing
Join row ends of front bib and main body together. Sew in base leaving an opening, fill, close opening. Gather cast on and cast off edges of head, fill (see picture). Sew head to body, with these tightly gathered points at each side. Gather ends of nose in the same way, fill and attach. Line ears and attach with cast on edges as the vertical, outside edge of each ear and with the base curved to give shape. Sew front paws into a sphere, fill and attach. Join tail seam matching stripes, fill and attach. Embroider features and sew on whiskers.

Dragon puppet

Because dragons are imaginary creatures, you can make them in all kinds of colours and decorate it in any way you wish. Puppets are great fun for children, and the one on page 81 will be a favourite.

Materials
Sirdar Wash 'n' Wear Crepe Double Knitting, part balls in green, dark turquoise, pale turquoise and yellow; small quantities of yarn of white and orange; oddments of yarn for embroidery; pair of 4mm/No 8 knitting needles; washable polyester toy filling.

Measurements
Approx 12in (30cm) long and 5½in (14cm) wide.

Tension
24 sts and 30 rows to 4in (10cm) measured over st st on 4mm/No 8 needles.

Back (make 1)
Using green, cast on 33 sts.
Beg k row and working in st st, work until back measures 8in (20cm).
Dec 1 st each end of next, then every foll 3rd row until 15 sts rem.
Cast off.

Belly (make 1)
Using dark turquoise, cast on 33 sts.
Beg k row and working in st st stripes of 4 rows dark turquoise and 4 rows pale turquoise, work until belly measures 8in (20cm).
Keeping stripe pattern correct, dec 1 st each end of next, then every foll alt row until 15 sts rem.
Cast off.

Mouth (make 1)
Using yellow, cast on 15 sts.
Beg k row and working in st st, inc 1 st each end of first, then every foll alt row to 33 sts.
Dec 1 st each end of every foll 3rd row to 15 sts.
Cast off.

Tongue (make 1)
Using orange, cast on 20 sts.

Next row: Cast off 10 sts, k to end.
Next row: P.
Next row: Cast on 15 sts, cast off 15 sts, k to end.
Next row: P.
Next row: Cast on 10 sts, cast off all 20 sts.

Eyes (make 2)
Using dark turquoise, cast on 1 st.
Working in st st, work as follows:
Next row: Work 4 times knitwise into this st.
Next row: P.
Next row: Inc 1 st in every st – 8 sts.
Work 4 rows.
Change to yellow and work 3 rows, so ending p row.
Next row: (K2 tog) to end – 4 sts.
Next row: P.
K4 tog, fasten off.

Back spikes (make 2 in each of yellow, pale turquoise and dark turquoise)
Cast on 8 sts.
Working in garter st (k every row), dec 1 st each end of every 4th row until 2 sts rem.
K2 tog, fasten off.

Teeth (make 4)
Using white, work as for back spikes, but cast on only 6 sts.

Finishing
Join straight sides of back and belly together. Sew in mouth matching shapings. Sew down a line either side of the centre of the lower jaw to accommodate the wearer's thumb. Sew on spikes by their cast on edges in a line down the centre back. Sew on eyes, lightly padded with filling. Sew on teeth by their cast on edges, then sew in tongue. Embroider eye centres, lids and nostrils (see picture).

Big Jumbo

Elephants have been beloved toys with generations of children. This cuddly Jumbo is so appealing, you will want to knit him again and again.

Materials
3 (50g) balls Sirdar Country Style Double Knitting in grey; small quantity in each of white and dark grey; oddments of yarn for embroidery; pair of 4mm/No 8 knitting needles; washable polyester toy filling.
Measurement
Approx 14in (36cm) tall.
Tension
24 sts and 30 rows to 4in (10cm) measured over st st on 4mm/No 8 needles.

Main body piece (make 1)
Using grey, cast on 12 sts.
* Working in st st, work as follows:
Next row (wrong side): P.
Next row: Inc knitwise in every st – 24 sts.
Next and every alt row: P.
Next k row: (Inc knitwise in next st, k2, inc knitwise in next st) 6 times – 36 sts.
Next k row: (Inc knitwise in next st, k4, inc knitwise in next st) 6 times – 48 sts.
Next k row: (Inc knitwise in next st, k6, inc knitwise in next st) 6 times – 60 sts.
Cont in this way, inc 12 sts on every alt row, until there are 144 sts *.
Work 43 rows straight, so ending p row.
Next row: (K2 tog, k20, k2 tog tbl) 6 times – 132 sts.
Next and every alt row: P.
Next k row: (K2 tog, k18, k2 tog tbl) 6 times – 120 sts.
Next k row: (K2 tog, k16, k2 tog tbl) 6 times – 108 sts.
Cont in this way, dec 12 sts on every alt row until 24 sts rem.
Next row: P.
Next row: (K2 tog) to end – 12 sts.
Run a thread through rem sts.

Legs (make 4)
Using grey, cast on 40 sts.
Beg k row and working in st st, work straight for 4½in (11cm).

Cast off loosely.

Foot base (make 4)
Using dark grey, cast on 8 sts.
Beg k row and working in st st, inc 1 st each end of first 2 rows, then foll alt row – 14 sts.
Work 8 rows straight.
Dec 1 st each end of next, then foll alt row – 10 sts.
Dec 1 st each end of the next row – 8 sts.
Cast off.

Head (make 1)
Using grey, cast on 12 sts and work as given for main body piece from * to *, but only until there are 96 sts.
Work 39 rows straight, so ending p row.
Next row: (K2 tog, k12, k2 tog tbl) 6 times – 84 sts.
Using this as a foundation row, dec 12 sts on every foll alt row in the same way as the main body piece until 36 sts rem, so ending k row.

Trunk
Next row: K.
Next row: K.
Next row: P.
Next row: K.
Rep the last 4 rows 15 more times (64 pattern rows in all), **at the same time**, dec 1 st each end of every 4th row until 24 sts rem, working straight when dec is completed.
Cast off.

Ears (make 2)
Using grey, cast on 36 sts.
Beg k row and working in st st, work 4in (10cm) straight, ending k row.
Next row: K.
Beg k row, work a further 4in (10cm) straight.
Cast off.

Tusks (make 2)

Using white, cast on 12 sts. Beg k row and working in st st, dec 1 st each end of every 4th row until 2 sts rem. Work 2 tog, fasten off.

Finishing

Join body seam leaving an opening, fill, then close opening. Join side edges of legs and insert a foot base in one end of each leg, fill and attach open ended. Join head and trunk, matching shaping and pattern on trunk seam and joining the trunk end flat, fill, filling the trunk and attach. Double ears at reversed row and join sides. Attach with a deep fold to give shape. Join tusk seams, fill and attach. Make a plaited cord tail, attach and tassel the free end. Embroider toe nails and eyes (see picture).

Tiger

Tigers are one of the most beautiful of animals, and are becoming increasingly rare. This stripey character is essential in your toy jungle.

Materials
1 (50g) ball Sirdar Country Style
Double Knitting in yellow; small quantity
in each of black and white; oddments of
yarn for embroidery; pair of 4mm/No 8
knitting needles; washable
polyester toy filling.

Measurement
Approx 5½in (14cm) high at the shoulder.

Tension
24 sts and 30 rows to 4in (10cm) measured
over st st on 4mm/No 8 needles.

Main body piece (make 1)
Using yellow, cast on 6 sts.
Working in st st, work as follows:
Next row (wrong side): P.
Next row: Inc knitwise in every st – 12 sts.
Rep these 2 rows until there are 48 sts.
Next row: P.
* Change to black and work 2 rows.
Change to yellow and work 6 rows *.
Rep from * to * 6 more times.
Change to black and work 2 rows.
Change to yellow and work 2 rows, so
ending p row.
Next row: (K2 tog) to end – 24 sts.
Next row: P.
Rep these 2 rows until 6 sts rem.
Run a thread through rem sts.

Belly (make 1)
Using white, cast on 2 sts.
Working in st st, work as follows:
Next row (wrong side): P.
Next row: Inc knitwise in every st – 4 sts.
Rep these 2 rows until there are 16 sts.
Work 61 rows straight, so ending p row.
Next row: (K2 tog) to end – 8 sts.
Next row: P.
Rep these 2 rows until 2 sts rem.
Work 2 tog, fasten off.

Head (make 1)
Using yellow, cast on 8 sts.
Working in st st, work as follows:
Next row (wrong side): P.
Next row: Inc knitwise in every st – 16 sts.
Next and every alt row: P.
Next k row: (Inc knitwise in next st, k2, inc knitwise in next st) 4 times – 24 sts.
Next k row: (Inc knitwise in next st, k4, inc knitwise in next st) 4 times – 32 sts.
Next k row: (Inc knitwise in next st, k6, inc knitwise in next st) 4 times – 40 sts.
Cont in this way, inc 8 sts on every alt row, until there are 56 sts.
Next row: P.
Work as given for main body piece from * to * once.
Change to black and work 2 rows.
Change to yellow and work 2 rows.
Next row: (K2 tog, k10, k2 tog tbl) 4 times – 48 sts.
Next and every alt row: P.
Next k row: (K2 tog, k8, k2 tog tbl) 4 times – 40 sts.
Next k row: (K2 tog, k6, k2 tog tbl) 4 times – 32 sts.
Cont in this way, dec 8 sts on every alt row until 16 sts rem.
Next row: P.
Next row: (K2 tog) to end – 8 sts.
Run a thread through rem sts.

Muzzle (top half, make 1)
Using yellow, cast on 24 sts.
Beg k row and working in st st, work 10 rows.
Next row: (K2 tog) to end – 12 sts.
Next row: P.
Next row: (K2 tog) to end – 6 sts.
Run a thread through rem sts.

Muzzle (lower half, make 1)
Using white, cast on 12 sts.
Beg k row and working in st st, work 10 rows.
Next row: (K2 tog) to end – 6 sts.
Next row: P.
Next row: (K2 tog) to end – 3 sts.
Run a thread through rem sts.

Ears (make 2)
Using yellow, cast on 7 sts.
Beg k row and working in st st, work 6 rows straight.
Dec 1 st each end of next row – 5 sts.
Change to white and inc 1 st each end of next row – 7 sts.
Work 6 rows straight.
Cast off.

Legs (make 4)
Using white, cast on 7 sts.
Next row (wrong side): P.
Next row: Inc knitwise in every st – 14 sts.
Work 3 rows.
Next row: K4, inc knitwise in next 6 sts, k4 – 20 sts.
Change to yellow and work 7 rows.
Next row: K4, (k2 tog) 6 times, k4 – 14 sts.
Work 12 rows straight.
Cast off.

Tail (make 1)
Using yellow, cast on 24 sts.
Beg k row and working in st st, work 6 rows.
Work as given for main body piece from * to * 6 times in all, so ending p row.
Next row: (K2 tog) to end – 12 sts.
Next row: P.
Next row: (K2 tog) to end – 6 sts.
Run a thread through rem sts.

Finishing
Join body seam leaving an opening, fill, close opening. Sew on belly patch centrally over the seam without further filling. Join leg seams, fill and attach open ended. Join tail seam matching stripes, fill lightly and attach with top end flat. Join head seam, matching stripes. Join together lower and top halves of muzzle by their side edges, leaving cast on edges free, fill and attach open ended to centre of front of head by these cast on edges. Fill and attach head. Double ears, join edges and attach. Embroider claws, eyes, mouth, nose and lines to define each side of the nose. Sew on white whiskers (see picture).

Embroider the tiger's eyes, mouth and nose (see pages 20 and 40). Define the nose with straight stitches

Work whiskers by bringing yarns through to front in position. Make two small stitches in same place to secure, cut yarn end

Snake

Toy snakes can be any size and children love to drape them around their shoulders, or coil the body on the floor to make a comfortable place for them to sit. You could also make the snake long enough to fit across a door, to keep out the winter draughts.

Materials
Sirdar Country Style Double Knitting, part balls in each of yellow (Y), beige, darker green (D) and brighter green (B); small quantity of Double Knitting in red; oddments of yarn for embroidery; pair of 4mm/No 8 knitting needles; washable polyester toy filling.

Measurement
Approx 40in (102cm) long.

Tension
24 sts and 30 rows to 4in (10cm) measured over st st on 4mm/No 8 needles.

Main body piece (make 1)
Using D, cast on 3 sts.
Beg k row and working in st st, inc 1 st each end of every 5th row until there are 17 sts. Work 1 row, so ending p row.
Cont to inc each end of every 5th row as before until there are 31 sts, **at the same time** work in pattern from the chart with next row as row 1 of chart.
Place the pattern centrally as shown, working all 20 rows of chart, then repeating rows 3 to 20 only, so working a central band up the work of diamond shapes on 9-row alternate stripes of the two greens.
When there are 31 sts, work straight in pattern until snake measures approx 35in (89cm), ending row 9 of pattern.
Pattern a further 2 rows, but do not introduce D or the new diamond at either side, so ending with a complete central diamond and k row in B.
Cont in B throughout.

Shape head:
Next row: P.
Next row: K1, (inc knitwise in next st, k1) to end – 46 sts.
Work 17 rows straight, so ending p row.
Next row: K1, (k2 tog, k1) to end – 31 sts.
Work 13 rows straight, so ending p row.
Next row: K1, (k2 tog) to end – 16 sts.
Next row: (P2 tog) to end – 8 sts.
Run a thread through rem sts.

Belly (make 1)
Using beige, cast on 3 sts.
Beg k row and working in st st, inc 1 st each end of every 10th row to 17 sts.

Work straight until belly is ⅜in (1cm) shorter than the complete length of the back, ending p row.
Next row: K1, (k2 tog) to end – 9 sts.
Next row: P1, (p2 tog) 4 times – 5 sts.
Run a thread through rem sts.

Eye bumps (make 2)
Using D, cast on 5 sts.
Working in st st, work as follows:
Next row (wrong side): P.
Next row: Inc knitwise in every st – 10 sts.
Work 3 rows straight.
Change to Y and work 4 rows straight.
Next row: (K2 tog) to end – 5 sts.
Run a thread through rem sts.

Finishing
Join main body piece and belly evenly together, matching any shaping and leaving an opening, fill and close opening. Fill and attach eye bumps. Embroider eye centres and nostrils. Make and attach a plaited or twisted cord red tongue.

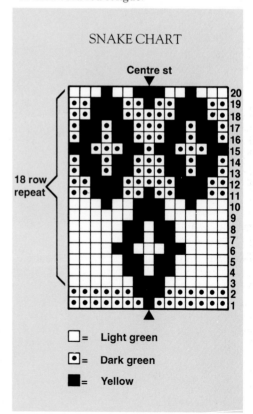

SNAKE CHART

Centre st

18 row repeat

20
19
18
17
16
15
14
13
12
11
10
9
8
7
6
5
4
3
2
1

☐ = Light green
⊡ = Dark green
■ = Yellow

PARROT

Materials
Sirdar Wash 'n' Wear Crepe Double Knitting, small quantities in each of yellow, turquoise, royal blue, red and grey; oddments for embroidery; pair of 4mm/No 8 knitting needles; washable polyester toy filling.

Measurement
Approx 8in (20cm) long.

Tension
24 sts and 30 rows to 4in (10cm) measured over st st on 4mm/No 8 needles.

Main body piece (make 1)
Using turquoise, cast on 5 sts.
Working in st st, work as follows;
Next row (wrong side): P.
Next row: K1, inc knitwise in next 4 sts – 9 sts.
Next row: P.
Next row: Inc knitwise in every st – 18 sts.
Rep the last 2 rows once more – 36 sts.
Work 17 rows, so ending p row.
Next row: (K2 tog) to end – 18 sts.
Next row: P.
Rep the last 2 rows once more – 9 sts.
Next row: K1, (k2 tog) to end – 5 sts.
Run a thread through rem sts.

Head (make 1)
Using turquoise, cast on 20 sts.
Beg k row and working in st st, work 10 rows.
Next row: (K2 tog) to end – 10 sts.
Next row: P.
Rep the last 2 rows once more – 5 sts.
Run a thread through rem sts.

Wings (make 2)
Using royal blue, cast on 4 sts.
Beg k row and working in st st, inc 1 st each end of every row to 10 sts.
Work 4 rows.
Change to red and work a further 8 rows.
Dec 1 st each end of next, then every alt row until 2 sts rem.
Work 2 tog, fasten off.

Wing linings (make 2)
Work as for wings, but work in yellow throughout.

Chest patch (make 1)
Using red, cast on 8 sts.
Beg k row and working in st st, work 4 rows.
Change to yellow and work 8 rows.
Dec 1 st each end of next 2 rows – 4 sts.
Cast off.

Eye patches (make 2)
Using yellow, cast on 3 sts and inc 1 st each end of next row – 5 sts.
Work 3 rows.
Dec 1 st each end of next row – 3 sts.
Cast off.

Beak (make 1)
Using grey, cast on 16 sts.
Next row: K.
Next row: P.
Next row: (K2 tog, k4, k2 tog tbl) twice – 12 sts.
Next row: P.
Next row: (K2 tog, k2, k2 tog tbl) twice – 8 sts.
Cast off.

Tail back (make 1)
Using red, cast on 4 sts.
Beg k row and working in st st, work 2 rows.
Inc 1 st each end of next, then every foll 10th row until there are 10 sts.
Work 9 rows, so ending p row *.
Dec 1 st each end of next, then every foll alt row until 2 sts rem.
Work 2 tog, fasten off.

Tail front (make 1)
Using royal blue, work as for tail back to *.
Cast off.

Finishing
Join body seam leaving an opening, fill, then close opening. Join sides of head, fill and attach by cast on edge, open ended to top of body. Join linings inside wings and attach, without filling by their top, blue, edges only. Attach chest patch without filling, immediately below head. Join tail front to lower part of tail back, matching shaping, fill lightly and attach open ended so that point at top of tail back matches centre back and top of tail is central on the bottom of the body. Join beak, fill and attach. Attach eye patches without filling. Embroider feet, claws, beak line, nostrils and eyes (see picture on page 91).

Hippo

Hippopotami are delightful to knit and make very good nursery friends because they are such strong characters and yet cuddly and comfortable.

Materials

2 (50g) balls Sirdar Wash 'n' Wear Crepe Double Knitting in grey; small quantity in pink; oddments of yarn for embroidery; pair of 4mm/No 8 knitting needles; washable polyester toy filling.

Measurement

Approx 7½in (19cm) tall.

Tension

24 sts and 30 rows to 4in (10cm) measured over st st on 4mm/No 8 needles.

Main body piece (make 1)

Working in st st, work as follows:
Using grey, cast on 7 sts.
* **Next row (wrong side):** P.
Next row: Inc knitwise in every st * – 14 sts.
Rep from * to * until there are 112 sts.
Beg p row and working in st st, work 59 rows, so ending p row.
** **Next row:** (K2 tog) to end.
Next row: P ** – 56 sts.
Rep from ** to ** until 7 sts rem.
Run a thread through rem sts.

Legs (make 4)

Using grey, cast on 32 sts.
Beg k row and working in st st, work 12 rows.
Work as given for main body piece from ** to ** until 8 sts rem.
Run a thread through rem sts.

Head (make 1)

Using grey, cast on 80 sts.
Beg k row and working in st st, work 20 rows.
Next row: (K2 tog) to end – 40 sts.
Work 19 rows, so ending p row.
Shape nose:
Next row: K10, inc knitwise in next 20 sts, k10 – 60 sts.
Work 7 rows, so ending p row.
Next row: K10, (k2 tog) 20 times, k10 – 40 sts.
Next row: P.
Next row: (K2 tog) to end – 20 sts.
Cast off.

Lower jaw (make 1)

Using grey, cast on 20 sts.

Beg k row and working in st st, work 8 rows.
Dec 1 st each end of next 4 rows – 12 sts.
Change to pink and inc 1 st each end of next 4 rows – 20 sts.
Work 8 rows.
Cast off.

Tail (make 1)

Using grey, cast on 9 sts.
Cast off.

Ears (make 2)

Using grey, cast on 6 sts.
Beg k row and working in st st, work 4 rows.
Dec 1 st each end of next row – 4 sts.
Change to pink and inc 1 st each end of next row – 6 sts.
Work 4 rows.
Cast off.

Eye bumps (make 2)

Using grey, cast on 24 sts.
Beg k row and working in st st, work 4 rows.
Next row: (K2 tog) to end – 12 sts.
Next row: (P2 tog) to end – 6 sts.
Run a thread through rem sts.

Finishing

Join body seam, leaving an opening, fill, then close opening. Join leg seams, fill and attach open ended. Join head seam matching shaping and doubling the cast off edge into a horizontal seam so that the main seam will be central under the head, leave the cast on edge of the head open, fill and attach centrally to end of body by this cast on edge. Double jaw, join edges and attach centrally, without filling below the nose. Seam eye bumps, fill and attach open ended. Double ears, join edges and attach with base folded to give shape. Attach tail. Embroider eyes, nostrils and whisker dots (see picture).

You may sometimes be tempted to buy odd balls of yarn in sales for making knitted toys. You can be successful doing this but make sure you buy a comparable yarn to that specified in the pattern and always knit a tension square on the recommended needles before starting to knit.

For my parents, G.T. and Harry.

Acknowledgement

All the yarns in this book were kindly
supplied by SIRDAR plc. In event of
difficulty obtaining yarns please write to:

SIRDAR plc
Flanshaw Lane
Alverthorpe
Wakefield
West Yorks WF2 9ND